Good, bad and amaz[...]
most of us just don[...]

101
AMAZING
PEOPLE
THAT WE ONLY KNOW ABOUT BECAUSE WE
REDDIT

Dan Brady
Ruth Lunn
Ursula Harris
Ruth Davis
Samuel Peters

U K Book Publishing.com

First published in Great Britain in 2014

Copyright © 2014 UK Book Publishing

Editing, design and publishing by UK Book Publishing

UK Book Publishing is a trading name of Consilience Media

Whitley Bay, Tyne and Wear NE26 2SB UK

www.ukbookpublishing.com

ISBN: 978-1-910223-26-0

Neither the authors nor UKbookpublishing.com are in any way affiliated with reddit.com

Contents

CRIME 109

Introduction

As the title suggests, the idea for the book was inspired by the website reddit.com

In case you aren't familiar with reddit, let me explain a little. It's the self-styled 'home page of the Internet', founded in the US in 2005 by Alexis Ohanian and Steve Huffman. reddit's basic premise is simple – anyone can submit a link to anything on the web, and anyone else can up vote, down vote or comment on it. The result is an ever-changing chart of user-generated content and discussion, and it rarely fails to be interesting or entertaining.

At the time of writing, a typical month sees 174 million unique visitors to reddit, and over three million active, logged in users. There are over six billion pages in total on the site, and rising.

One of the many recurring themes on reddit is links to stories of people who've done incredible, wacky, brilliant or even dumb things. For instance, the mother who performed a caesarean on herself, the bank robber who thought lemon juice would make him invisible, and the scientist whose breakthroughs have probably saved a billion lives. These and many more are brought together here.

History is full of people like this who've done

amazing things – some incredibly courageous, others heinous, and yet more skirting at either end of the spectrum known as 'luck'.

In an age where many celebrities are famous for doing very little, it's perhaps ironic that these remarkable people – whether good or bad – haven't become better-known. This book is one small effort to bring a few of those people that have the most interesting, yet little-known stories to a wider audience, and to generally marvel at what some people get up to.

A cynic might suggest that this book is an attempt to turn procrastination into productivity (reddit is notorious for losing hours of your life), but I couldn't possibly comment on that.

Enjoy discovering some new amazing people.

Dan Brady
/u/AlDente
November 2014

PS This book is not affiliated with reddit, we are just fans and users. If you like what you read here, I suggest you take a look at the site, especially the subreddits (topics) 'todayilearned', 'bestof', 'nottheonion' and 'truereddit'.

Acknowledgements

Huge thanks to everyone who has made this book a reality, especially contributors Ruth Lunn, Ursula Harris, Ruth Davis, Samuel Peters, Kimberley Bell and the UKbookpublishing.com team including Jay Thompson and Judith Barker.

Thanks most of all to the reddit users who continue to contribute amazing content to the site each day. Stay classy, reddit.

Listed in the next section are the reddit users whose links first alerted us to the people and stories in this book.

Big thanks to these reddit users

This book wouldn't exist without the reddit users you see listed on these two pages. It was their posts and comments that led us to discover the stories contained in this book. Each story is credited individually too, unless a user account has been deleted.

3ofspades
5kl
AbeltonSkive
Aboly
ActualStack
aeo1003
Allformygain
axolotl_peyotl
Battle4Seattle
Bekaloha
blackstar9000
cmd194
costheta
Count_Bruno
Darrkman
Dildo_Ball_Baggins
DrRichardCranium

earthtoannie
fallenseraphim
free_potatoes
godsenfrik
gramturismo
grendel001
hinesh
IAMAnarcissist
imbignate
interpellation
IoCarry
jaundicedave
JeffreyGlen
JordanLeDoux
Kamon2011
lappy482
last0nethere

LegendaryBlue
lfairy
lilygal
linkittogether
liverman
LonginiusSpear
Lonzy
marquis_of_chaos
megster53
michaeldunworthsydne
mosestrod
ndyrg2
neshalchanderman
Ninja_OT
Ninjabackwards
NMW
pilgrim_soul
potato1
puffdamgcdrgn
rino23
SamadhiBlue
scientologist2
segaliberationarmy
seven7hwave
ShakaUVM
sirmaxwell90

Ska-doosh
SlantmentEnchantment
slapyomamah
SledDave
SnugNinja
SoberAenima
someguyfromcanada
SonnyBlack90
spellbreaker
Squeenis
Streeb-Greebling
SweatyBaws
Tamnegripe
TeleSavalas
thebobstu
TheCannon
themetz
thesoulcrusher
timopod5
tmos1985
tomega
TryHardDieHard
Webguy55
Wrestlingisgood
YesIAmYou

"Don't wait for permission to be awesome."

– *Alexis Ohanian, co-founder of reddit*

HISTORY

"History will be kind to me for I intend to write it."

– Winston Churchill

Thomas Midgley

"More impact on the atmosphere than any other single organism in Earth's history"

Thomas Midgley was a smart chemist and engineer who held over 100 problem-solving patents. Lauded in his lifetime, his legacy is now distinctly tarnished, as it was he that introduced two chemicals which have had catastrophic effects on public health and the environment: leaded gasoline and Freon, the first CFC.

In the early twentieth century, the automobile had arrived, and engineers were constantly trying to improve internal combustion engine technology. Pressures in the engines were increased to gain extra power and fuel efficiency, but an unintended side-effect was a common problem known as 'knock'. This manifested as a loud 'knocking' sound, as well as engine damage and uneven performance. The problem affected all internal combustion engines of the time, including aircraft.

Whilst working for the General Motors Research Corporation, Midgely sought to solve the problem. He discovered that the increased heat and pressure in the engine cylinder caused the fuel and air to burn unevenly. He then experimented with many fuel additives in order to create an 'anti-knock' fuel which would burn evenly.

Several additives were found to be effective, but

were rejected due to reasons such as cost, corrosiveness and even smell. Eventually, in 1921 Midgley settled on tetra-ethyl lead (TEL) as the ideal additive. Lead was attractive as not only were very small quantities effective in preventing 'knock', but it was cheap and easy to refine. With his team, Midgley worked through 1922 to perfect the TEL additive recipe.

Awareness of the dangers of lead was growing, however. Lead poisoning had long been associated with seizures, blindness, kidney failure, brain damage, mental illness, coma and death. But public awareness and general safety standards were poor. Lead was used in toys, food containers, paint, and many other household items. In 1922, the League of Nations (a precursor to the United Nations) recommended a ban on interior lead paints due to health concerns. Europe complied, but the United States did not.

Leading scientists wrote to Midgley, to deter him from using the "creeping and malicious poison" of tetra-ethyl lead, often citing its role in the death of researchers, and calculating the amounts of lead that would be released to the atmosphere and deposited on roads and cities. Their warnings were ignored.

In December 1922, the US Surgeon General wrote to General Motors, expressing growing concerns that lead would become a serious public health issue. Midgley replied that TEL pollution had been given "very serious consideration," but that "the average street will probably be so free from lead that it will be impossible to detect it or its absorption". Ironically, Midgley was about to spend the winter in Miami to treat his own mild lead poisoning. Nevertheless, nothing would dampen his enthusiasm for tetra-ethyl lead.

Marketed as *Ethyl*, the lead-based fuel additive product went on sale in 1923. Soon after, the Indianapolis 500 race was dominated by cars running on Ethyl gasoline, demonstrating its effectiveness and resulting in a rapid growth in the fuel additive's popularity.

Even as sales took off though, questions remained about the safety of lead additives in fuel, so, in October 1924 Midgley participated in a press conference to demonstrate TEL's safety. In the demonstration, he poured TEL over his hands, then placed a bottle of the chemical under his nose and inhaled its vapour for 60 seconds. He declared that he could do this every day without succumbing to any problems.

A few months later, Midgely travelled to Europe for lead poisoning treatment. Even this didn't change his thoughts on the matter. In a paper presented to the American Chemical Society in 1925, Midgley contradicted his own earlier work by stating that "tetraethyl lead is the only material available that can bring about these (antiknock) results". Use of lead additives in fuel continued to grow, unabated.

By the mid-1930s, around 90% of all US gasoline contained lead-additives. In 1936 the US Federal Trade Commission issued a restraining order preventing commercial criticism of lead-based fuel additives, stating that leaded fuel was "entirely safe to the health of motorists and the public ... is not a narcotic in its effect, a poisonous dope, or dangerous to the life or health of a customer, purchaser, user or the general public". It would be decades until this official line was recanted.

In 1930, Midgely was tasked with another problem. Gases used in refrigerators and air conditioners were highly toxic and explosive, and Midgley was asked to find an odour-free, non-toxic, and non-flammable alternative.

Midgley and his team experimented with alkyl halides (combinations of carbon chains and halogens). Establishing a pattern of apparent disregard for public health concerns, they rejected the assumption that these compounds would be toxic. The team eventually created dichlorodifluoromethane, the first chlorofluorocarbon (CFC), which they named 'Freon'. Freon and other CFCs soon replaced the various toxic or explosive substances previously used as refrigerants, and were later used in other applications, such as propellants in aerosol spray cans and asthma inhalers. Although safer than previous refrigerants, the effect that CFCs would have on our planet's atmospheric ozone layer would only be discovered decades later.

For his chemical breakthroughs he received four medals from the American Chemical Society, including the Perkin Medal in 1937, and election to the National Academy of Sciences.

Meanwhile, despite deaths and lead poisoning of tetraethyl workers, and some temporary Ethyl factory closures, use of lead-based fuel additives continued to increase. By the early 1960s, almost all US gasoline contained lead-based anti-knock additives. By this time, engineering progress meant that the mechanical need for lead was no longer required – knocking could be eliminated without it. But lead was big business, and enjoyed federal protection. When one manufacturer offered an unleaded gasoline alternative without the need for 'dangerous chemicals', the lead-additive industry sued, and won.

The tide started to turn when another remarkable person, Dr Clair Patterson, began to research the causes of lead in the atmosphere and environment. In 1965 Patterson devised a new method to compare historical levels of atmospheric pollutants – he took core samples from ice in Greenland, and measured the lead content of each layer. Using this technique he proved that atmospheric lead had been negligible before 1923, and levels had grown sharply from that point on. At the time of the tests, lead levels were roughly 1,000 times higher than they had been in the pre-Ethyl era. He also found that modern humans' bone lead levels were hundreds of times higher than pre-1923.

Patterson was offered lucrative roles in the lead industry, which, to his great credit, he declined. He was ostracised in the scientific and legislative communities, but didn't give up. His pioneering work eventually led (pun intended) to the 1970 US Clean Air Act.

TEL was not regulated as a pollutant in the US until 1977. Around the same time, catalytic converters had begun to be introduced to capture other toxic emissions from cars. Coincidentally, lead additives prevented the catalytic converters from functioning, so their use instigated the phasing out of lead in fuels.

By 1986, lead-based additives were virtually eliminated in the United States. As a result, between 1970 and 1997 total lead emissions fell from 199,000 to 3,600 tonnes per year.

Midgley's work resulted in huge quantities of lead being released into the atmosphere via the combustion of leaded gasoline all over the world.

Studies have associated links between high atmospheric lead levels and serious long-term health problems, including neurological impairment. Airborne lead has also been linked to rates of violence and criminality in cities. Researchers have discovered very close correlations between levels of childhood lead exposure and crime data in cities in the 1990s, in Australia, Canada, Great Britain, Finland, France, Italy, New Zealand and West Germany – in other words, every country they looked at. In the US states where consumption of leaded gasoline declined slowly, crime declined slowly too. Conversely, in states where it declined quickly, crime also declined quickly.

Although the use of lead has dropped significantly, its effects are likely to persist. Researchers in 1998 extended Patterson's research. Despite levels falling, they found that atmospheric lead levels are still several hundred times higher than the natural levels they found in samples over 6,000 years old.

Plus, lead hasn't been completely eradicated as an emission. Leaded fuel is still used in some aircraft, and in automobiles within some third-world countries. A few industrial processes also expel lead as a waste product.

It might seem unfair to judge Midgley using our present-day knowledge of the health and environmental impacts, but – particularly with lead – he was given ample evidence of its devastating effects. Not least, personally.

Midgley didn't live to see the effects of his work. Aged 51, he contracted polio, which resulted in him losing the use of his legs. The system he designed to lift himself into and out of bed was the eventual cause of his own death when he was entangled in the ropes and died of strangulation at the age of 55, in 1944.

J R McNeill, an environmental historian, has remarked that Midgley "had more impact on the atmosphere than any other single organism in Earth's history".

reddit referrer: pilgrim_soul

Alexei Ananenko, Valeri Bezpalov and Boris Baranov

Three men who saved Europe from becoming a radioactive wasteland

The Chernobyl disaster is infamous as the worst nuclear power plant accident in history. But few people are aware that its effects would have been far worse, if it wasn't for the selfless actions of three brave men.

For nearly two days after the disaster, no one was warned about the radiation, as those in charge were desperate to hide the truth. Workers and firefighters fought courageously to put the fire out, but none were told the dangers. Even when the levels of radiation became obvious, they continued.

Immediately after the explosion, thousands of gallons of water had been pumped into reactor 4 in a futile attempt to extinguish the fire. This flooded the reactor's basement, but couldn't stop the burning.

Several levels above the water, the reactor was melting. A chamber housing a huge piece of radioactive graphite and fuel had reached 1200°C and was melting through the concrete floor.

If this radioactive lava had come into contact with the water below, it would have caused a massive steam explosion, with thousands of tons of radioactive material being ejected into the atmosphere. It was likely that this would also have triggered further nuclear explosions in the three other nearby reactors. The effects would have been almost unimaginable. Hundreds of square miles of Europe would have been uninhabitable for centuries, and the global death toll would have increased significantly.

After six days the melting of the reactor could not be halted, so to prevent it coming into contact with the flooded basement, it was essential that the huge pool of water was drained. But to drain the pool required swimming through the flooded basement – which was by now filled with intense, lethal radiation.

The men knew this was a suicide mission. Nevertheless, Alexei Ananenko, Valeri Bezpalov and Boris Baranov volunteered, knowing that their actions would save the lives of many thousands. All three donned scuba gear and swam through the flooded chambers of the basement and opened valves to allow the 20,000 tonnes of radioactive water to drain out.

The men managed to swim back to their cheering co-workers, but died soon after leaving the power plant.

As with all who died at Chernobyl, Ananenko, Bezpalov and Baranov were buried in lead coffins. We can only guess at how many lives they saved.

reddit referrer: BabycakesJunior

Alayne Fleischmann

Whistleblower of the financial crisis

Alayne Fleischmann's experience of working at the heart of the US financial system gives a rare insight into exactly the kinds of deals and trading that led to the 2007/2008 financial crisis. And her evidence led to the largest regulatory fine in US history – a whopping $13 billion.

Canadian-born Fleischmann joined JPMorgan Chase in 2006 as a diligence manager – essentially a quality control officer to ensure the company avoided bad loans. After just a few months working at the bank, Fleischmann began to experience problems with her boss. She later testified to the United States Department of Justice that her manager had instructed Fleischmann and others in the firm to not email him. "If you sent him an e-mail, he would actually come out and yell at you," she said. "The whole point of having a compliance and diligence group is to have policies that are set out clearly in writing. So to have exactly the opposite of that – that was very worrisome."

A key aspect of the diligence team's responsibilities was to assess the risk of 'securities' – tradable financial assets. Later in 2006 Fleischmann and others in her diligence team were tasked with evaluating a $900

million security – a package of home loans that had
originated from GreenPoint Mortgage. The diligence
team immediately spotted that many of the package's
loans had 'suspiciously' old dates. Ordinarily, banks wish
to produce securities from loans as quickly as possible,
ideally within two to three months; however, the loans
from GreenPoint were seven or eight months old. The
diligence team interpreted this as an indicator that the
deal had already been rejected by a bank, or else were
'early payment defaults' or EPDs (loans that had been
previously sold to another institution and had been
returned after the borrowers had defaulted on several
payments).

When Fleischmann and her team reviewed a random
sample of loans in the GreenPoint package, they found
that many were based on incomes that were overstated.
Fleischmann recalled that one debtor was a manicurist
who claimed to have an income of $117,000 a year –
more than five times the US national average. Chase's
typical tolerance level for overstated income within a
loan package was 5%, but the diligence team judged
that approximately 40% of the Greenpoint package had
overstated income.

Knowing that debtors would be likely to default on
many of the loans, Fleischmann informed her managers.
But instead of rejecting the GreenPoint package,

managers pressured the diligence team to change their reports so that only 10 per cent of pool's loans were recorded as problematic. This was still twice the usual acceptable 'overstated income' level, so Chase lifted its threshold to allow the deal to progress.

Following a meeting where these issues had been raised, Fleischmann approached Greg Boester, a managing director at Chase, and warned him that Chase was about to commit fraud.

In early 2007 Fleischmann wrote a letter to another Chase managing director, warning of problems with the GreenPoint deal, and the consequences of selling bad loans as good. Regardless, executives at Chase went ahead and approved the GreenPoint loan package. They could now sell the loan package as securities to their customers.

As the 2007 financial crisis exploded, Greenpoint Mortgage was an early casualty. Just a year after being bought by Capital One for $13.2 billion, the unit was now shut down.

In February 2008, with the banks in meltdown, Fleischmann was fired as part of a series of layoffs.

Not long afterwards, Chase CEO Jamie Dimon boasted in an interview with *Fortune* to have known as early as 2006 that the subprime mortgage market was being wrongly valued and not given accurate risk levels. By January 2010, when asked to testify before the Financial Crisis Inquiry Commission, Dimon was telling this story in a different light. In this new version, Dimon claimed that Chase directors had been oblivious to problems in the home loan markets: "In mortgage underwriting," he said, "somehow we just missed, you know, that home prices don't go up forever."

By 2012, Fleischmann had moved back to Canada, when she received a phone call from the US Securities & Exchange Commission (SEC) – one of the organisations that had recently been tasked with investigating the causes of the financial crisis. She told the SEC about the GreenPoint deal, but initially they were only interested in another suspicious, but smaller, Chase deal. Eventually, attention turned to the GreenPoint deal, and Fleischmann became hopeful that her evidence would bring some of the Chase directors to be held criminally accountable for their actions.

On September 24th 2013, a press conference was organised to publicise the charges against Chase. But on the morning the event was suddenly cancelled and no complaint was filed.

Writing in Rolling Stone, investigative journalist Matt Taibbi described what happened:

It goes without saying that the ordinary citizen who is the target of a government investigation cannot simply pick up the phone, call up the prosecutor in charge of his case and have a legal proceeding canceled. But Dimon did just that. "And he didn't just call the prosecutor, he called the prosecutor's boss," Fleischmann says. According to The New York Times, after Dimon had already offered $3 billion to settle the case and was turned down, he went to Holder's office and upped the offer, but apparently not by enough.

... Fleischmann later realized that the government wasn't interested in having her testify against Chase in court or any other public forum. Instead, the Justice Department's political wing, led by Holder, appeared to be using her, and her evidence, as a bargaining chip to extract more hush money from Dimon. It worked. Within weeks, Dimon had upped his offer to roughly $9 billion.

The final deal cost JPMorgan Chase $13 billion, with the US Justice Department proclaiming it the largest settlement with a single entity in American history.

The media jumped on the story; some voices claiming a triumph for the Government, and others bemoaning government over-penalisation of banks.

However, the settlement wasn't quite as straightforward as the $13 billion figure indicated. For starters, the deal comprised $9 billion in cash, with $4 billion classed as 'consumer relief', presumably to make the amount seem greater.

"$4 billion of the settlement was largely an accounting falsehood, a chunk of bogus consumer relief' added to make the payoff look bigger," Taibbi explained. "What the public never grasped about these consumer-relief deals is that the 'relief' is often not paid by the bank, which mostly just services the loans, but by the bank's other victims, ie, the investors in their bad mortgage securities."

Fleischmann was equally scathing of the consumer relief aspect of the Chase deal: "It's not real, they structured it so that the homeowners only get relief if they would have gotten it anyway. If a loan shark gives you a few extra weeks to pay up, is that 'consumer relief'?"

In addition, Chase was allowed to treat $7 billion of the settlement as a tax write-off. When news of the settlement was announced, the bank's share price soared six per cent, adding more than $12 billion in value to shareholders. In 2013, to save costs and protect margins, Chase shed 7,500 employees.

The deal released Chase from civil litigation, but not from criminal liability.

Fleischmann waited for the Justice Department to file criminal charges against Chase directors. "How is it possible that you can have this much fraud and not a single person has done anything criminal?" Fleischmann told CNBC.

But in a speech in September 2013, Justice Department Attorney General Eric Holder suggested it is unlikely that charges will ever be made: "Responsibility remains so diffuse, and top executives so insulated," Holder said, "that any misconduct could again be considered more a symptom of the institution's culture than a result of the willful actions of any single individual."

Fleischmann expressed her frustration: "I think the difficulty is the country has been told that this was all an accident or there's no evidence to go forward on this; there is a mountain of evidence. There are emails. There are reports. There are external reports. There's testimony from other employees. So I think the concern is when this can happen and it can get written off as just 'we didn't know what we were doing', then you can see this happening again."

And what of CEO Jamie Dimon, the man who oversaw the biggest regulatory penalty that the US has ever known? The JPMorgan Chase board awarded him a 74 per cent raise, and increased his compensation package to about $20 million.

reddit referrer: neshalchanderman

Diane Hartley

Student who saved a New York skyscraper from collapsing

At 915 feet, the Citigroup Center's 59 storeys stand prominently on the New York skyline. However it was not always certain that the skyscraper would still be standing today. The architect behind the project was Hugh Stubbins, but the chief structural engineer, William LeMessurier, was the man in charge of making the building safe and able to withstand the tests of time. And it was LeMessurier who was responsible for constructing the building on four stilts.

The skyscraper's unusual nine-storey stilts were incorporated into the building's design when it became apparent that St Peter's Lutheran Church – which stood in one corner of the building site – had to be accommodated. However, with the stilts came several issues, mostly concerning the stability of the structure. In order to balance 50 storeys on nine-storey stilts, LeMessurier fashioned a building which would rise in rows of eight-storey chevrons. Although the chevron design helped balance the building, it also made the structure so light that it would visibly sway in high winds. To combat this problem, LeMessurier added a 400-ton damper to the design, a device which would weigh down the skyscraper and stabilise it.

Satisfied that the high-rise structure would stand sturdily on its spindly legs, construction went ahead. In 1978, only a year after the Citigroup Center was finished and opened to the public, a civil engineering student from Princeton University, Diane Hartley, who had been studying the skyscraper for her undergraduate thesis, contacted LeMessurier to tell him that the Center was unsafe.

During her research, Hartley had discovered that while the structure accounted for winds hitting all sides of the building, it hadn't factored in winds hitting the corners, called quarterly winds. LeMessurier looked into the claims himself and found the student's research to be correct. Further studies of weather data told him that winds strong enough to topple the Citigroup Center hit New York every 55 years, and that in the event of a power cut – which would stop his 400-ton damper from working – there was a statistical risk of the skyscraper collapsing once every 16 years.

The shocking discovery came in June at the start of the hurricane season and LeMessurier had to act immediately. However, with his reputation at stake if the mistake became publicly known, he decided to conduct all repairs under the cover of darkness. Six weeks into the emergency repairs, workers frantically spent whole nights welding huge steel plates onto the bolted corners of the building as the news arrived that Hurricane Ella was heading swiftly towards New York. Just hours before a ten-block radius around the building was due to be evacuated, the crucial stablising repairs were still only half-finished.

Luckily for LeMessurier, Hurricane Ella changed course before it reached New York and his reputation remained intact for almost 20 years because, conveniently for him, the New York Times had been on strike during the emergency works on the Citigroup Center.

It wasn't until a writer called Joe Morgenstern overheard the tale at a party and published the story in the New Yorker in 1995 that the critical condition of the skyscraper became known. Diane Hartley, the student whose undergraduate thesis had brought attention to the instability of the Center, only became aware of how crucial her research had been in preventing the collapse of the Citigroup Center when she saw a documentary aired on the BBC, 20 years after she had raised her concerns.

There is little doubt that Hartley's thesis saved the lives of hundreds of New Yorkers.

reddit referrer: ActualStack

Henry Dunant

Humanitarian hero who created the Red Cross and won a Nobel Peace Prize

Born in 1828, the son of a wealthy Swiss family, Henry Dunant could be said to be the perfect accidental hero. A college drop-out, Dunant turned his hand to business, and soon found himself on the cusp of an exciting, if troublesome business deal in French colonial Algeria. Determined not to be beaten, Dunant made plans to appeal to Emperor Napoleon III in person for aid. In 1859, armed with a flattering book he had written about the emperor, Dunant travelled to Italy to meet him.

However, when Dunant arrived in the small Italian town of Solférino, it coincided with the immediate aftermath of the bloody Italian second war of independence. Rather than the imperial aid he sought, Dunant instead found a war zone – and with it, his true lasting legacy.

Roughly 300,000 soldiers had fought at the Battle of Solférino – the last major battle in world history where all the armies were under the personal command of their monarchs. Dunant was confronted, he later wrote, by "chaotic disorder, despair unspeakable, and misery of every kind" as soldiers, Italian, French and Austrian, lay in the mud, bloodied, dying, unaided.

Aghast, Dunant immediately sprang into action, organising a voluntary force of young women from Solférino to administer basic first aid, which, he later noted, extended as far as applying olive oil and bandages. Over the next days and weeks, Dunant organised a number of makeshift hospitals, made plans for the care of the injured, and eased the suffering of the dying.

Deeply moved by his experiences, Dunant wrote his second and most famous book, *Un Souvenir de Solférino* (*The Memory of Solférino*). Using his own money to fund publishing, and family contacts to distribute, *The Memory* soon had as many as 1,600 copies distributed across the world.

The book had three key features: the details of the battle itself, the despair of the battlefield Dunant discovered, and crucially, a plan for change. Here Dunant laid the foundations for the sweeping reforms that would change the battlefield for good. Nations were urged to form relief societies, paid for by a governing board of national leaders, to care for the wartime wounded. Care was to be provided by volunteers, who, unlike in Solférino, were to be trained, funded and well equipped. And all this was to be done under the Solférino inspired catchphrase, '*Tutti fratelli*' ('All are brothers').

So it was that the world began to change, under

the influence of a mediocre businessman. On the 7th February 1863, the Geneva Society for Public Welfare was created. A board of five were elected, including Dunant, and the plans of *The Memory* discussed in earnest. From there, the humanitarian movement began. Dunant travelled the world, meeting with dignitaries and organising an international organisation to put his plans into action. By October 1863, 16 nations had met, discussed and approved several sweeping reforms. By August that same year, 12 nations had signed an international treaty creating a humanitarian armada, a voluntary force, under the flag of a red cross, on a plain white background. The Geneva Convention was born, and with it, the Red Cross.

But Dunant was not yet finished. The Geneva Convention had given birth to the Red Cross, but Dunant was determined to give it strength. Within months, the organisation's responsibilities extended to cover naval forces. Later, the Red Cross became the face not only of wartime humanitarian aid, but also of peacetime aid, taking control of humanitarian relief efforts during periods of natural disaster.

At this point, Dunant's luck changed. In 1867, the humanitarian giant was brought back to earth with a crash, his company falling into administration. Dunant himself was bankrupted, accused of financial misdealing, and ostracized by Swiss society. His place on the humanitarian main stage removed, Dunant was sacked, replaced, and humiliated. For the next 20 years, Dunant embraced the obscurity and poverty he had been threatened with as a college drop-out, forgotten by the world.

It was not until 1895 that the world remembered the name Dunant – by now an old man, ill in his hospice. Dunant was awarded the world's first Nobel Peace Prize, finally acknowledging his work in founding the International Red Cross and initiating the Geneva Convention.

It was too little, too late, however. Hurt by the cruelty of the world, Dunant died in his hospice in Heiden, his last words being "Where has humanity gone?".

As a final act of charity, Dunant dedicated his estate (including the Nobel Prize money which he had not spent) to charitable organisations and the funding of a 'free bed' in the Heiden nursing home – to be made available for a poor citizen of the region.

Henry Dunant lived a life of true contrast. Born to a wealthy family, he fell to financial despair. A college drop-out, he changed the world for good. The Nobel Prize committee stated: "There is no man who more deserves this honour... Without you, the Red Cross, the supreme humanitarian achievement of the nineteenth century, would probably have never been undertaken".

Dunant's birthday, 8 May, is celebrated each year as the World Red Cross and Red Crescent Day.

reddit referrer: marquis_of_chaos

Masabumi Hosono

Surviving the Titanic disaster led to a life of shame and misery

Masabumi Hosono was the only Japanese passenger aboard the Titanic. His decision to survive by taking a place on a lifeboat was later condemned by the Japanese government and public, who thought it would have been more honourable for him to go down with the ship.

The 41 year old civil servant was on his way back from Russia, where he had been researching the railway system, when he boarded the Titanic at Southampton. Hosono was a second class passenger, but assumed to be third because he was the only passenger of his race on board, meaning when the ship started to sink, he was initially prevented from going to the boat deck. When he was finally able to reach it, the emergency flares showed the imminence of the disaster. His thoughts turned to his wife and children, as the lifeboats were filling up rapidly. When an officer shouted that there was 'room for two more' on lifeboat ten, another man jumped aboard, and Hosono followed suit. Due to the dark night and the sight of the sinking ship, the men in charge of the boat did not realise there were two men aboard.

Hosono bore the brunt of taunts by officers on the RMS Carpathia, which carried the survivors to New

York. From America, he was able to travel back home to Japan, where he was interviewed by many Japanese magazines and newspapers.

However, this publicity led to public condemnation, both in Japan and America, as he was thought of as a 'stowaway' and rumours circulated about him dressing up as a woman in order to gain a place on the lifeboat.

Hosono lost his job, and was thought of as 'immoral' by many. There have been varying theories as to why he was so negatively thought of, but most observers comment that his actions were viewed as having disgraced Japan.

Hosono never spoke of the matter himself, and even after his death it remains a source of shame for his family.

But Hosono wasn't the only Titanic survivor to be made to feel guilty.

J Bruce Ismay, president of the company which built the Titanic, was also on the ship that fateful day. He too suffered condemnation after taking one of the few lifeboat places as the ship was sinking. The decision to limit the number of lifeboats which the Titanic held was credited to Ismay, thus intensifying the vilification he suffered. On returning to England, Ismay received hate mail, had intense nightmares, and was disowned by the majority of his friends.

reddit referrer: Bekaloha1

Robert Smalls

The slave who sailed his way to freedom, and became a captain in the process

Born in April 1839, to the oppressive regime of The Confederate States, Robert Smalls' family could only have guessed at the gleaming future in front of him. A favourite of the household, Smalls' story began in earnest during his teenage years, at the household whipping post. There he watched his fellow slaves get beaten, and learned the true evils of the society into which he had been born. The lesson gave rise to a rebellious streak, and he was soon moved to Charleston and put to work, in an attempt to keep his mischief at bay.

It was some years later, during a post on the now famous SS Planter, that Smalls' legacy truly began. By then a married man with two children, Smalls feared for the future of his family, and, unable to pay the price set by their masters, hatched a plan for their escape, later dubbed '...*hazardous in the extreme*' (according to a Union Naval Committee report.)

An able seaman, with an uncanny likeness to the white captain of the ship, one Captain Rylea, Small made plans to look for an opportunity to exploit his skills and make good his escape to the more liberal American Union, whose naval blockade of the Confederacy

signalled for the captives a shining beacon of freedom
and hope, adorning the horizon just beyond their grasp.

Opportunity finally arose, one early May morning
in 1862. The Captain had moored the Planter for the
night in Charleston dock, taking the executive decision
to grant his crew a night of relaxation. Leaving the slaves
aboard, Rylea naively concluded that no harm could
come in a single night, promised his early return, and
went to join his family. There, alone in the darkness, a
ship ready for the taking, Smalls could at last smell his
freedom. He shared his plan with the slaves aboard,
hatched over the past sea voyage, took his place on deck,
and urged the Planter out of dock, and on to freedom.

The plan was simple, dangerous, and the result
of ingenuity that only the hope of freedom can bring.
Banking on an uncanny likeness to Captain Rylea,
the low light of early morning, and the straw hat the
Captain had left on deck, Smalls planned to pose as
the Captain himself, and sail under a flag of truce to
the safety of the Union blockade. To do so, however, he
would need to pass three Confederacy guardhouses, and
approach in full view a naval force ready and able to
blow his Confederacy ship apart. Yet freedom alone is
not freedom at all, and with this in mind, Smalls added
a further dangerous element to his plan. He intended
also to pick up his wife, his two small children, and

several other slaves in need, carrying them to safety, all in view of their masters and under the watchful eye of the Confederacy Navy.

So, in the silence of an early morning, Smalls set off with his crew of six slaves, his straw hat, and his ingenuity. Relying on a lack of visibility, Smalls pulled the large straw hat over his face, crossed his arms as he had seen the Captain do a hundred times, and began his voyage. An hour later, and in full view of a Naval guardhouse, he docked, welcomed his loving family aboard, and made way. So far, so good.

Two more guard houses were passed, each staffed with naval administration. With the coolness of an iron nerve, Smalls delivered the correct naval whistle greeting to each house, as calmly as if the Captain had done so himself, crossed his arms, and bowed his head, and allowed his straw hat to hide the genius of his plan. Confederate flags raised in defiant deception, the Planter edged its way to the horizon that promised a new life. Smalls and his crew were under no illusions. Capture meant certain death, and they were prepared. Guns loaded and desperate for freedom, the slaves lay in wait for detection.

But it never came. As early morning gave way to the first light of dawn, red sun glowing on the waters that carried them to freedom, Smalls, his crew and his family, approached the Union blockade. As they sailed at last, with a sigh of relief, out of range of Confederation guns, the alarm was sounded. But it was too little, too late; freedom was calling.

There was but one last challenge to overcome – the Union guns. Quickly, Smalls called for the Confederation flags to be removed, only to be replaced with a white bed-sheet, serving as a flag of truce. Having promised all runaways a new life in the Union, this bed-sheet, taken from the bed of the very masters that had enslaved his family, allowed Smalls and his passengers safe passage to a new life beyond the blockade.

Yet Smalls was still not finished. He quickly signalled to the leader of the blockade, and there delivered the SS Planter, with its armaments and equipment, over to the Union. Later, the Union blockade was to write of Smalls: "…Robert is superior to any who have come into our lines – as intelligent as many of them have been."

Not only had Smalls earned his freedom, and captured a Confederation ship, he was also able to provide the Union with valuable information. So impressed were the Union leadership with Smalls' heroic achievements that they paid him $1,500 for the capture of the SS Planter. And, following his lobbying for the right of black men to join the Union army, allowed him to recruit for the Union cause, which he achieved with admirable aplomb.

Our story ends with a final act of bravery, and the true commendation that Smalls deserved. The SS Planter was returned to the water, this time fighting for the Union, with the one and only Captain Robert Smalls at its head. Over a military career of more than 17 engagements, under heavy fire and against the odds, Smalls became one of the highest ranked and best paid officers in the Union Navy. The final poetic flourish of this heroic tale brings us back to Charleston Harbour. The Union victorious, Smalls was able to return home a free man, the truest Captain the SS Planter had ever had.

reddit referrer: someguyfromcanada

Lord Nithsdale

Escaped from the Tower of London dressed as a woman

The Tower of London was a formidable prison for many in centuries past; however, a guise of cross-dressing helped a Scottish aristocrat escape in 1716.

Catholic William Maxwell, Fifth Earl of Nithsdale, was arrested after being involved in riots as a protest against the then-recent taking of the English throne by Protestant King George of Hanover.

On hearing of her husband's arrest, Lady Nithsdale knew execution would be likely, so travelled from Scotland to London in order to aid him in an escape plan.

Accompanied by her maid and a friend by the name of Miss Hilton, Lady Nithsdale went to the Tower to visit her husband. She had realised that many people passed through the Tower daily by no organised system, with guards who were not overly strict, as they were happy to be tipped discreetly.

An extra cape was worn by Miss Hilton, so as not to arouse suspicion by being seen carrying it. The women aimed to confuse the guards with as much activity to and from the cell as possible, meaning initially Lady Nithsdale and Miss Hilton entered, then Miss Hilton left and the maid arrived, but did not enter the cell.

Lady Nithsdale then proceeded to disguise her husband by rouging his cheeks, painting out his eyebrows and covering him in scarves so that his beard could not be seen. After being dressed in the extra riding cape, which Miss Hilton had left, Lord Nithsdale was led out of his cell in the fading afternoon light. He kept his head down, under the pretence of crying, and was passed to the maid, who left with the Tower with him. Lady Nithsdale then returned to the cell, and continued to speak in a low voice, as if to her husband, imitating his replies. When she finally left, she requested the guards leave her husband for a while, as he was praying before hearing his sentence the next morning. After leaving, Lady Nithsdale made for Mrs Mills' rooms in Drury Lane, where Lord Nithsdale was hiding. He was then hidden in the house of the Venetian ambassador, and from there escaped to France, disguised as a coachman. His wife later joined Lord Nithsdale in France, and they lived the remainder of their lives in exile there.

On hearing of the escape, King George's alleged response was "for a man in my Lord's situation, it is the very best thing he could have done!".

reddit referrer: ShakaUVM

AMAZING FEATS

*"Only those who attempt the absurd
can achieve the impossible."*

– Albert Einstein

Bertold Wiesner

Sperm donor extraordinaire

The Barton Clinic championed artificial insemination in London in the 1940s. Set up by Austrian-born Bertold Wiesner and his wife Mary Barton, the clinic controversially used a small number of highly intelligent men as sperm donors.

The clinic helped women conceive more than 1,500 babies, but in recent years it became apparent that many of the babies were not in fact fathered by donors, but were the offspring of Bertold Wiesner himself.

It was known that Weisner was a donor, and apparently Mary Barton had limited the 'number of donations' that he would make. But ultimately Weisner was responsible for sourcing donors.

In 2007, DNA tests were carried out on 18 people who had been conceived at the clinic between 1943 and 1962. Results showed that 12 were Wiesner's children.

Estimates of the number of offspring fathered by Wiesner range between 600 and 1,000. If the true figure is at the higher end of the range, this makes Wiesner second only to seventeenth century Moroccan emperor Moulay Ismaïl for the number of children fathered.

reddit referrer: LonginiusSpear

Moulay Ismaïl 'the Bloodthirsty'

Father of over 1,000 children

Moulay Ismaïl Ben Chérif was a ruler of the Moroccan Alaouite dynasty, for over fifty years starting in the late seventeenth century. Known as a fearsome leader, Moulay Ismaïl was responsible for fighting off the Ottomans, expelling the English and Spanish from Moroccan territory and expanding the Moroccan empire. He even claimed to be a descendant of Muhammad.

His reputation as 'bloodthirsty' arose when he had the heads of 10,000 enemy soldiers displayed on the walls of Meknes, the capital city. Meknes had been built at Ismaïl's command, using at least 25,000 slaves. There are many accounts of Ismaïl having slaves beheaded. During the 20 years of Ismail's rule, it is estimated 30,000 people died.

But perhaps Moulay Ismaïl's most remarkable feat was his alleged fathering of over 1,000 children.

By 1703, a total of 867 children, including 525 sons and 342 daughters, had been recorded. In 1721 his 700th son was born.

Apparently only the daughters of Ismaïl's four wives were allowed to live — hence the lower total number of daughters. And his most 'senior' wife allegedly controlled who he slept with, the scheduling of which must have kept her busy to say the least.

With over 1,000 children by the time he died in 1727 at the age of 80, Ismaïl is widely considered to have had the largest verifiable number of offspring for any man throughout history. And had all the daughters been allowed to live, the figure would have been significantly higher.

Modern-day scientists have studied the case of Moulay Ismaïl in order to determine whether there are limits to male fertility, and whether it could have been feasible for him to sire so many offspring. The general consensus appears to be that, yes, it is (and was) feasible.

Note: for a close second, see Bertold Wiesner in the previous story.

reddit user: user's account no longer active

Nicholas Alkemade

Fell 18,000 feet without a parachute, and survived

Amazingly, there are a number of confirmed accounts of people surviving high altitude falls from aircraft. During World War II there were several such incidents, but the one we've chosen to include here is perhaps the most interesting.

Flight Sergeant Nicholas Stephen Alkemade (1923-1987) was a rear gunner in the British Royal Air Force's heavy bombers during World War II.

One night in March 1944, 21-year-old Alkemade was in an Avro Lancaster bomber, part of a 300-strong bomber raid on Berlin.

Whilst returning from the raid, Alkemade's bomber was attacked by the Luftwaffe, caught fire and began a deadly spiral. Finding that his parachute had been damaged by the fire in the aircraft, and with few options in a now-plummeting aircraft, Alkemade was left with a grim choice – die in the plane or jump to his death without a parachute. He decided to jump, preferring to die by impact rather than burn to death, and fell 18,000 feet (5,500m) to the ground below.

"I thought well, this is the end," he told French filmmakers, decades later. "Rather than stay here and burn to death, I'll bail out and make a quick end of it.

So I rotated the turret by hand, flipped open the doors.
Didn't even bother to disconnect my intercom, I just
bailed straight out. I seemed to be falling headfirst; it was
very peaceful. And I thought, 'well, if this is dying, there's
nothing to it, there's nothing to be afraid of'."

Alkemade was lucky, to say the least. His fall was
broken by pine trees and a deep snow cover on the
ground. When he regained consciousness, he was covered
in multiple lacerations and bruises, but was able to move
his arms and legs and incredibly his most serious injury
was merely a sprained leg.

Two of the Alkemade's crew members were able to
parachute from the plane, but the remaining four were
not so fortunate. The Lancaster crashed, killing pilot
Jack Newman and three others – they are buried in the
Commonwealth War Graves Commission's Hanover War
Cemetery.

When Alkemade realised he was alive, and not badly
injured, he lit up a cigarette and reflected on what had
just happened. "I had enough pieces of tree in my body
to start a bonfire," he said, "but I was alive, and I walked
away."

But he didn't walk to freedom. Alkemade was
captured by the Gestapo, who initially thought him to
be a spy, as they didn't believe his story of surviving a
fall without a parachute. But when the wreckage of the

aircraft was discovered and examined, it corroborated his story, and Alkemade became a celebrated prisoner of war. The Germans even gave him a certificate authenticating the miraculous fall. Alkemade was repatriated back to Britain in May 1945, and later worked in the chemical industry.

> Note: *another incredible free fall survivor of WWII was Alan Magee of USA. In 1943 he survived a 22,000-foot (6,700m) fall by crashing through the glass roof of the St Nazaire railway station in France. Though severely injured, the Germans gave him medical treatment, and he survived.*
>
> reddit referrer: Streeb-Greebling

Philippe Petit

French tightrope walker who walked between the Twin Towers in New York

Philippe Petit first stepped onto a tightrope wire at the age of 16 in his home town of Nemours, France. It didn't take long for him to fall in love with the art, and in just a year he had taught himself to perform every trick in the book on the wire – a year in which he was also expelled from no fewer than five schools.

In 1968, aged 17, Petit read an article about the proposed construction of the World Trade Center in New York, and knew straight away that he wanted to perform there. However the actual performance didn't happen until six years later. Not only did Petit have to wait until the towers themselves had been built, but he had to do some extensive research so that he would be able to sneak into the building, reach the rooftop unnoticed by security, and shoot a 200kg steel wire across the 61 metre gap to the opposite tower.

Over the years of planning, Petit visited New York several times to assess the towers and plan his performance. This involved breaking into the building with his crew, spending whole nights hiding on the rooftops to learn about security measures and scouting out how to secure the equipment that would be needed for the endeavour. To practise for the World Trade Center walk, he rigged and walked a wire between the towers of Notre Dame, Paris in 1971 and two years later, walked between the two north pylons of Sydney Harbour Bridge.

Finally, on the night of 6th August 1974, disguised as workmen, Petit and his crew made it to the 104th floor and began setting up the high-wire. A fishing line was shot across the gap using a bow and arrow. Then, increasingly larger wires were attached to each other and hauled across until finally the steel wire itself was stretched out between the two towers.

Petit then set out across the wire, battling against high winds and the natural swaying of the towers, 1,350 feet above the ground. His performance lasted 45 minutes, during which time he crossed the 61 metre void eight times to the cheers of crowds a quarter of a mile below. Before the police managed to persuade him back to solid ground, threatening to pluck him off by helicopter, Petit danced, walked, knelt to salute the people below and lay down on the wire.

After the performance, Petit was let off all charges on the condition that he perform again for children in Central Park, which he did over Turtle Pond. He stayed in New York City after his achievement and was praised for bringing much needed commercialism to the Twin Towers, which had not at first been popular amongst the public.

Speaking to *The Guardian* in 2003, Philippe Petit said in response to people asking him whether he has a 'death wish', "After doing a beautiful walk, I feel like punching them in the nose. It's indecent. I have a *life* wish."

reddit referrer: JeffreyGlen

Thomas Fitzpatrick

Pilot who drunkenly landed a plane on a narrow street in northern Manhattan for a bet. Twice

Thomas Fitzpatrick, an ex-marine, became renowned amongst residents of northern Manhattan after he successfully landed a plane on St Nicholas Avenue outside the bar where he had been drinking with friends.

Fitzpatrick first took to the skies as a 26 year old on 30th September 1956, when he stole a plane from Teterboro School of Aeronautics in New Jersey, took off with neither lights nor radio communications, and made what The New York Times reported as "a fine landing" in the narrow, unlit street outside the Manhattan bar. Fitzpatrick later admitted that the flight was the result of a bet made between friends while they were drinking, which an eye-witness specified was "that he could be back in the Heights from New Jersey in 15 minutes".

The pilot accomplished this incredible feat not only once, but twice, when he felt compelled to fly again on 4th October 1958 after a bar patron wouldn't believe his first achievement. Fitzpatrick stole a plane from the same airfield, but chose a different street for his landing, touching down outside a Yeshiva University building on 187th Street.

For his first flight, the young pilot got away with a

mere $100 fine for violating the city's administrative code, which forbids the landing of a plane in the street. However for his second flight, Fitzpatrick was sentenced to six months in jail for bringing stolen property into the city. Fitzpatrick died in 2009, aged 79, but the legend of his two miraculous landings in the narrow streets of Manhattan live on in the memories of all those who woke to find a plane nestled between the parked cars and lamp-posts of their street.

reddit referrer: jaundicedave

Dashrath Manjhi

Love can move mountains

Dashrath Manjhi was a member of a labouring family who lived in the Indian village of Gahlour near Gaya. The Gehlour mountain hills meant the village was 70km from the nearest doctor, as a path had to be climbed through the hills in order to reach the nearest town. This location proved problematic when Dashrath's wife, Falguni Devi, was seriously injured in 1967. She required immediate medical treatment; however the length of the path meant the distance to the nearest doctor was so great that she could not receive the treatment required in time, and she passed away before adequate medical help could be reached. Dashrath was devastated at his loss, and more so at the reason for it. Consequently, he decided to dedicate his life to prevent others suffering the same tragic loss.

The location of Dashrath's village amongst the rocky hills between Atri and Wazirganj meant that even though the nearest town of Gaya was relatively close by, there was no straight path to it. Equipped with hammer, chisel and nails, Dashrath began the task of changing this by building a tunnel through the mountain. Despite the initial taunts of others, Dashrath's determination saw him daily continuing to work at creating the tunnel. The ridicule which others initially gave him merely served to enhance his determination to complete the task. As the tunnel began to materialise, attitudes changed and the local villagers supported Dashrath with offers of food and tools. In 1988, the task which had taken almost 22 years was completed, and a tunnel 360 feet long, 30 feet high and 25 feet wide provided access through the mountain. The distance between Atri and Warziganj was now a mere 15km path, meaning medical treatment could be accessed much more rapidly, benefiting all the inhabitants of the Gaya district.

The 'Mountain Man', as he became known, died in August 2007 as a result of gall cancer. However, his legacy continues: due to his work there was increasing awareness of the lack of adequate access from villages to nearby towns with healthcare professionals. As a result, the Chief Minister of Bihar proposed a 3km metalled road to be built between Gahlaur and Amethi, named the 'Dashrath Manjhi Road'. His work in serving the healthcare of his fellow villagers was also furthered as a hospital was set up for them, again in his name. There can be no doubt as to the significance of Dashrath's labour of love in improving access to healthcare for villagers in his area.

reddit referrer: thesoulcrusher

Don Ritchie

Former life insurance salesman who saved 160 people from suicide

'The Gap' is a cliff in Australia with a grisly notoriety stretching back to the nineteenth century. It's the country's most infamous suicide spot, with an average of one death per week.

So, you might imagine that living near 'the Gap' would be distressing. But not for former life insurance salesman Don Ritchie, whose house was just metres away from the cliff edge. Ritchie, who died in 2012 aged 86, for many years made a point of looking out of his window each morning for "anyone standing alone too close to the precipice". If he saw someone who looked like they might jump, he engaged them in conversation and often invited them back to his house for tea.

"I'm offering them an alternative, really," Ritchie said. "I always act in a friendly manner. I smile."

On occasions he physically restrained people from jumping while his wife Moya called the police. It's estimated that Ritchie and Moya saved more than 160 people from jumping to their death. Ritchie's efforts didn't save everyone, but he was philosophical, comforted that he had done his best: "I think, isn't it wonderful that we live here and we can help people?"

Shortly before his death, Don received the Local Hero Award for Australia in 2011. The National Australia Day Council said: "His kind words and invitations into his home in times of trouble have made an enormous difference... With such simple actions, Don has saved an extraordinary number of lives."

reddit referrer: Dildo_Ball_Baggins

Ioannis Ikonomou

A Cretan translator who comfortably speaks 32 languages

Ioannis Ikonomou, whose mother tongue is Greek, started learning English when he was just six years old. From that moment his love affair with languages began and once he had mastered English, he pursued German, closely followed by Russian, Turkish and Arabic in High School, before going on to study linguistics at the University of Thessaloniki. Now 46, he says he feels comfortable speaking an impressive 32 languages, including Chinese, Polish and Sanskrit.

His incredible ability has not gone unnoticed, and he now works as a translator for the European Commission and is responsible for the translation of classified Chinese documents into European languages, a task which Ikonomou is able to complete with ease.

During his PhD in Indo-European linguistics at Harvard University, Ikonomou also studied many of the ancient languages such as Greek, Latin, Sanskrit, Old Persian, Classical Armenian, Gothic, Pali, Old Church Slavonic, Hittite, Luwian, Oscan, Umbrian and Irish.

Iknonmou believes that anyone can learn a language and that it is only a case of falling in love with, and immersing oneself in, both the language and culture of a country. He is currently learning Amharic, the official language of Ethiopia and the oldest African language and, true to his own theory, is enjoying dining in Ethiopian restaurants whenever possible.

reddit referrer: JordanLeDoux

QUIRKY

*"I couldn't repair your brakes, so I
made your horn louder."*

– Steven Wright

Peter and Allison Cirioli

Second-born twin is the 'older' of the pair

Laura Cirioli, pregnant with twins, went into labour in November 2007.

Her first child – a son who she named Peter – was born at 1:32am. Thirty-four minutes later, Laura's daughter, Allison, was born. However, due to daylight saving, which in the US comes into effect on the first Sunday of November at 2:00am, Allison's recorded time of birth was 1:06am.

This peculiar twist made her 26 minutes 'older' than her brother, despite being born 34 minutes later.

reddit referrer: puffdamgcdrgn

Bill Morgan

Back from the Dead to Win the Lottery... Twice

When he was hit by a truck in 1998, Australian Bill Morgan's heart stopped beating for 14 minutes – he was clinically dead. Luckily for him, Morgan's heart started again, but he was now in a coma, and doctors suggested to his family that turning off life support was the best option. His family resisted, and 12 days later Morgan's luck returned as he regained consciousness and started to recover, with no sign of ill-effects.

One year later, Morgan proposed to the woman he had started dating after having 'died', and she said 'yes'. Morgan's lucky streak was starting to pick up steam. To celebrate his new-found good fortune, he bought a scratch card and was ecstatic to find he'd won a $17,000 car.

But Morgan's reversal of fortune hadn't ended yet. At a publicity event staged to deliver Morgan's new car and showcase his remarkable story, Morgan was asked to re-enact scratching his winning ticket. Morgan bought another scratch card from the same newsagent and won $250,000 right in front of the TV cameras.

"All these months I've had time to think about the heart attack and thank my lucky stars," he said later. "It was a worry even after I came out of hospital. But things

have gone so well – I got my old job back, I got engaged,
I won a car. It can't be true."

reddit referrer: free_potatoes

Charles Vance Millar

Canadian lawyer who bequeathed estate to whichever woman gave birth to most babies in ten years following his death

It sparked what became known as 'The Great Stork Derby' of the 1930s in Canada when wealthy lawyer Charles Vance Millar decided to leave his estate to the Toronto mother who gave birth to the most babies in the ten years following his death.

Millar, who had practised law in Toronto from 1881 until his death in 1926, had no close relatives to leave his money to, and had always enjoyed a perverse sense of humour, staging many practical jokes, in particular playing on others' greed and love of money.

As well as his earnings over the years, Millar had also made a number of investments, some of which proved prodigious, including shares in a tunnel being built from Windsor in Ontario to Detroit, Michigan. By the time the bequest was due to be paid, ten years after Millar's death, the investment in the tunnel had turned a $100,000 estate into one worth $750,000 – a highly significant sum in the days of the Depression, when the minimum wage was $12.50 for a 60-hour week.

The media kept up its interest over the ten year period, tracking the mothers who were in the race. In the meantime, the courts wrangled over the details of the will (deciding on questions such as whether stillborn children counted, or babies born to unmarried parents), and distant relatives of Millar also tried to claim their stake.

The result was a tie, with four women able to demonstrate nine properly registered live births. They received $125,000 each. Two other mothers who had given birth at least ten times, but did not meet the other criteria of live births or legitimacy, were given a settlement of $12,500 each.

Millar was well aware of his mischief. He said: "This will is necessarily uncommon and capricious because I have no dependents or near relations and no duty rests upon me to leave any property at my death and what I do leave is proof of my folly in gathering and retaining more than I required in my lifetime."

Folly for him, perhaps, but for 36 children who grew up in vastly improved financial circumstances, a real boon.

reddit referrer: scientologist2

Chuck Feeney

The billionaire who's given it all away

Chuck Feeney, arguably the world's poorest billionaire, is described by Forbes as "The billionaire who is trying to go broke". Born during the Great Depression in the unassuming blue-collar town of Elizabeth, New Jersey, Feeney was most certainly born without a silver spoon in his mouth. An Air Force veteran of the Korean War, Feeney's story truly begins in 1956, during his early entrepreneurial days as a self-made businessman, selling tax-free goods to sailors. With a flair for making money and the people skills to succeed, Feeney soon found himself running a small business, and it wasn't long before he was welcoming friends to the team, and looking to expand. In a matter of nine short years, Feeney had transformed his one-man business project into the large and successful *Duty Free Shoppers* (DFS) – boasting more than 200 employees and operating in more than 27 countries.

But there was more money to be made. In 1964, Japan lifted foreign travel restrictions on its citizens, and in so doing opened the floodgates for a tidal wave of rich Japanese tourists and travellers, eager to spend money saved up during more restricted times. Sensing the upcoming opportunity, Feeney made plans to expand

DFS, placing shops in areas likely to receive Japanese tourists, hiring Japanese workers and travel guides to encourage customers to shop there, and even building an airport to allow for a promising business location to receive more activity. Between 1967 and 1977 Feeney rocketed up from an annual pay of around $12,000 to a whopping $12 million, going on to bank roughly $334 million over the next decade.

Yet the most remarkable aspect of Feeney's life is not the money that he made, nor the way he made it, but rather the way he spent it. In 1988, Forbes named Feeney one of the richest men in America, running a four page exposé which suggested that the average DFS store earned a huge $20,000 per square foot, per year. By nature a private man, Feeney was distressed by the exposé.

But Forbes did not know, indeed many did not know, that the fortune attributed to Feeney did not actually belong to him at all. In 1984, Feeney had secretly transferred his entire 38.75% stake of DFS to the newly-created foundation 'Atlantic Philanthropies', thereby committing himself to a life of charitable giving that has gone to create his lasting legacy. Speaking to Forbes some years later, Feeney noted quite simply, ''I concluded that if you hung on to a piece of the action for yourself you'd always be worrying about that piece.''

Now in his mid-80s, Feeney is noted to have owned one second hand car in his life, to prefer Casio watches to Rolex, and to fly economy rather than first-class, if it meant getting to his destination at the same time. The life of luxury was never on the cards, Feeney notes, because, quite simply, he knew he wouldn't like it.

Instead, with Atlantic Philanthropies as his tool, Feeney has, over the past 30 years, dedicated himself to giving billions of dollars to charitable causes. With an entrepreneurial eye for maximising value, Feeney now prefers to take a personal interest in where his money is being spent, requiring in-depth business plans, requesting meetings with charity bosses, and taking a personal interest in maximising the effectiveness of every cent given. Feeney has been able to help organisations the world over, with projects including mending cleft-pallets in third world countries, building new facilities at universities across Ireland, and ensuring that research can be done by the best and brightest to bring innovation to the world. Feeney is also keen to play tough, in order to get other parties involved in his giving. In 1997, Atlantic Philanthropies proposed a $100 million donation to Ireland's universities to extend their facilities, but required the Irish government to match the donation before a single cent could be spent. Money-strapped though the government was, the deal was agreed. Since then, Feeney has been able to organise a total of $1.3 billion in government money for universities, alongside $226 million donated by Atlantic Philanthropies.

Perhaps most striking of all, however, is the secrecy that Feeney clung to, for as long as he was able. But with taking a clear personal interest in the works of the charities he helps to fund, Feeney has had to adapt his methods of working now that a degree of fame has found him. Yet he remembers fondly the earlier years of comforting obscurity, during which Atlantic Philanthropies was able to give to charities without them being entirely aware of where the huge sums were coming from. Speaking to Forbes, he noted with some amusement that organisations often had to be assured that mafia money was not involved, and that all donations were 'above board'. Those charities that were aware of his involvement were sworn to strictest secrecy.

Though Feeney mourns the loss of the obscurity that hid his philanthropy, fame has had its merits in the world of charitable giving. Both Bill Gates and Warren Buffett, two of the world's richest and most generous businessmen, credit Feeney as an inspiration for their own philanthropic efforts. Gates, famous for the $30 billion-endowed 'Bill & Melinda Gates Foundation', as well as for his involvement in the 'Giving Pledge', speaks fondly of Feeney, noting, "Chuck is fond of saying that none of us have all the answers… but I know that Melinda and I have learned a great deal from him in the time we've spent together."

As the world's poorest billionaire, Feeney has made a difference to lives the world over. A man from an unassuming background, with a flair for business and a competitive streak that took him to the top of his game, Feeney has encouraged some of the most valuable charitable exploits and important works in a variety of sectors in the last decade. Feeney encourages those in similar situations to do what they can. "People who have money have an obligation," he told Forbes. "I wouldn't say I'm entitled to tell them what to do with it but to use it wisely."

Feeney has given away almost all his fortune, apart from provisions for his four daughters and one son (while at college each worked regular jobs as waiters, maids and cashiers). Now in his eighties, Feeney is determined his foundation should spend all its funds in his lifetime. Atlantic Philanthropies plans to spend its remaining $1 billion endowment by 2016, with the total donated estimated to be over $7.5 billion.

Feeney told the New York Times in 2012, "I want the last check I write to bounce."

reddit referrer: SonnyBlack90

Ferdinand Demara

'The Great Impostor'

Ferdinand Demara pulled off some of the greatest identity hoaxes in history, so is probably better-known than many other people in this book. But we bet that many others haven't heard of him. Besides, his story is just too good to ignore.

Demara was born in Massachusetts, in 1921. Initially affluent, his family's fortunes worsened during the 1930s depression, and they were forced to move to poorer districts. Demara ran away from home aged sixteen.

He spent four years with Cistercian monks in Rhode Island, then joined the US Army in 1941. Not liking the army, he pretended to be another soldier and went AWOL. His habit of regular identity theft had begun, and after flirting again with monastery life, he then switched to the Navy. Unhappy with how his naval career was progressing, he faked suicide, and took the identity of Robert Linton French in order to become a religiously-oriented psychologist. He taught psychology at Gannon College in Pennsylvania, became an orderly in a Los Angeles sanitarium, and worked as an instructor in St Martin's College in the state of Washington. Eventually, he was apprehended by the FBI and he served 18 months in prison for military desertion.

After his release he joined the Brothers of Christian Instruction, a Roman Catholic order in Maine. This time he had already stolen another identity – Dr Cecil B Hamann, and was known by the order as 'Brother John'.

While there, Demara hatched a plan to promote the work of the religious teaching order by founding a college in Maine. Spearheading the effort himself, Demara managed to form the college and get it chartered by the state. He expected to be rewarded for his efforts with the Brotherhood appointing him as rector or chancellor of the new college, but in 1951 when this didn't materialise, he left the order. The college Demara founded, LaMennais College in Alfred, still exists today as Walsh University (now moved to Ohio).

While at the Brothers of Christian Instruction, Demara got to know a young doctor named Joseph C Cyr. Demara was impressed with Cyr's medical skills and, upon leaving the religious order, he chose to masquerade as Cyr. With this latest identity, the convincing Demara was welcomed with open arms by the Canadian Navy, and he soon found a role as a surgeon on a Royal Canadian Navy destroyer, HMCS Cayuga.

With the Korean War raging, the fake 'Cyr' was called to perform genuine surgery. Remarkably, despite no experience, he managed to improvise successful major surgeries, aided by the use of copious amounts of penicillin to ward off infections.

Following one battle, 16 South Korean combat casualties were loaded onto the Cayuga, for emergency treatment. As the only 'surgeon' on board, Demara was expected to save the lives of the badly-injured servicemen. To buy time, Demara ordered shipmates to prepare the injured for surgery. Meanwhile, Demara slipped off to his room with medical textbooks and proceeded to speed-read the surgeries he was now required to perform.

One casualty had a bullet lodged near his heart, and many of the ship's senior crew stood round as Demara began to operate. "I couldn't have been nervous, even if I felt like it," Demara later told LIFE magazine. "Practically everybody on the bloody ship was standing there, watching me."

Demara managed to remove the bullet, and save the man, to the cheers of the crew. Amazingly, none of the casualties died as a result of Demara's surgeries.

Nevertheless, Demara's exploits on HMCS Cayuga were to prove his downfall. A public information officer heard of the surgeon's exploits and decided to run a story and release it to the press. A Canadian newspaper covered the story, including a photo of surgeon 'Cyr'. The mother of the real Joseph Cyr read it, alerted the authorities, and officials notified Cayuga's Captain. So well regarded was the fake Cyr, that at first the Captain refused to believe that Demara was an imposter. But orders are orders, and Demara was sent back to Canada.

The Canadian Navy knew that Demara had enlisted under a false name, but they still assumed he was a real doctor – and he wasn't about to put them straight. Finally his fingerprints were checked and Demara's real identity was uncovered. No charges were pressed, but Demara was deported back to the United States.

On his return, Demara sold his story to LIFE magazine. In the article Demara claimed to have performed many other operations including amputations and the removal of a lung, during his time impersonating Dr Cyr.

A few years later, in 1960, a biography of Demara was published. *The Great Impostor*, by Robert Crichton, brought Demara's name and exploits to a wider audience. Demara's philosophy is explained by the following excerpt from the biography:

> *He had come to two beliefs. One was that in any organization there is always a lot of loose, unused power lying about which can be picked up without alienating anyone. The second rule is, if you want power and want to expand, never*

encroach on anyone else's domain; open up new ones.

*"I call it 'Expanding into the power vacuum',"
Demara proudly explains. "It works this way.
If you come into a new situation (there's a nice
word for it) don't join some other professor's
committee and try to make your mark by
moving up in that committee. You'll, one, have
a long haul and two, make an enemy." Demara's
technique is to find your own committee. "That
way there's no competition, no past standards
to measure you by. How can anyone tell you
aren't running a top outfit? And then there's
no past laws or rules or precedents to hold you
down or limit you. Make your own rules and
interpretations. Nothing like it. Remember it,
expand into the power vacuum!"*

Demara's fakery wasn't ended by the LIFE article and
biography, but his new-found fame made it much harder
to be an imposter. He adopted a new identity and started
work in a Texas prison, but – according to his biography
– he had to leave when an inmate came across the LIFE
magazine article. Moving to Penobscot Bay island, he
assumed the identity of a high school teacher named

Martin Godgart. When this ruse was discovered, it cost him six months in prison.

The 1961 movie, *The Great Impostor*, is loosely based on the biography of Demara's life story up until that point. In the movie, Demara was played by Tony Curtis.

Clearly a charismatic individual – during his life Demara became friends with many notable people, including a close friendship with actor Steve McQueen. Demara even delivered last rites to McQueen in November 1980.

Demara worked as a counselor and chaplain in the 1960s and 1970s. Complications from his diabetic condition required both of his legs to be amputated. He died due to heart failure in June 1982, at the age of 60.

He made very little financial gain from his deceptions. When asked to describe his motives, Demara is said to have replied: "Rascality, pure rascality."

reddit referrer: gramturismo

Greg Packer

Associated Press are tired of interviewing him

Gregory F Packer is a retired American highway maintenance worker from Huntington, New York. He is well known in news circles for his apparent obsession with being quoted as a "man on the street" in newspapers, magazines and television broadcasts.

More often than not, if there's a global or celebrity event in the New York area, Packer has made sure he's there. His goal is being first in line, and getting mentioned in press coverage.

He has been quoted as a member of the public in more than 100 articles and television broadcasts. According to the Nexis database, between 1994 and 2004 Packer was quoted or photographed at least 16 separate times by the Associated Press, 14 times by Newsday, 13 times by the New York Daily News, and 12 times by the New York Post.

He always gives his real name, but has admitted to fabricating stories and quotes to get into the paper or on TV. Over the years he's claimed to be a fan of American Football teams Pittsburgh Steelers, New York Giants and the Philadelphia Phillies – depending on which team had won that year.

According to the Columbia University Journalism

School: "He was first in the line to see ground zero when the viewing platform opened at the World Trade Center site December 30, 2001. He was the first in line in 1997 to sign the condolence book at the British consulate when Princess Diana died. He slept outside in the snow in Washington, DC in January 2001 to be the first in line to greet President George W Bush after his inauguration."

Packer was first in line again to purchase an iPhone at the Apple Store at Fifth Avenue in New York. He began camping in front of the store at 5am on Monday, June 25, 2007, 110 hours before the iPhone went on sale. He performed a similar stunt at the same Apple Store for the release of the iPad, but lost first position in line due to not having a reservation.

This led Silicon Alley Insider to label Packer as "the same stupid guy who's first in line for everything".

In a 2013 interview with *The New Yorker*, Packer stated that "The first time I saw my name in print, I couldn't believe that I made a major newspaper. That made me feel that I accomplished something". He also expressed disapproval at the directives issued by various news organisations to not quote him, saying, "If I'm their source for an interview, I don't see where the problem is at all. What I do is not only helping reporters do their jobs, but it's also helping me tell my family and friends where I've been. So it's a case of helping each other."

Despite his notoriety in news rooms, Packer is still managing to get quoted by the press.

reddit referrer: SlantmentEnchantment

Jason Thomas

The 'lost' hero of 9/II

When the twin World Trade Center towers collapsed in New York on 9th September 2001, almost everyone inside was killed.

Unbeknownst to rescue teams, two Port Authority police officers were seriously injured but still alive, trapped 30 feet below the rubble. After hours underground, with darkness falling, and no sign of rescue, the two men began to think they would die.

Conditions in the immediate aftermath were extremely dangerous, and the official searches for survivors had been suspended. Two US marines were working as volunteers with the rescue effort. They had been searching continuously for hours, without finding any survivors. Despite the official search being suspended, they carried on looking.

Eventually, the trapped police officers heard a man shout "US Marine Corps – can anybody hear me?". After the police officers responded, the marines climbed down and saved them.

The marine who first found the trapped police officers disappeared without a trace. His identity remained a mystery.

Five years later, Oliver Stone's movie of this rescue –

'World Trade Center' – was released, and trailers for it were airing on US TV. Watching one of these adverts was former marine, Sgt Jason Thomas. He quickly realised that the film was about himself.

Deeply affected by the incidents of 9/11, Thomas had not told anyone what had happened that day. Seeing the movie trailer prompted Thomas to confide in his family, who urged him to contact the film's producers.

In the movie, Sgt Thomas' character is played by a white actor. Oliver Stone and the producers of the 'World Trade Center' movie had not known that the 'missing marine' was black. Thomas has never seen the film.

Jason Thomas' remarkable story was featured in a 2013 UK Channel 4 TV documentary, '9/11: The Lost Hero', featuring interviews with Sgt Thomas, the rescued Port Authority police officers, and other eyewitnesses.

When Thomas joined the US Marine Corps, he learned to "Never leave your brother on the battlefield".

Talking to ebony.com, Thomas said, "I got lost for 15 minutes driving into the city. That baffled me because I knew how to get there. I wanted to get there sooner… Had I arrived 15 minutes earlier, I would have been in the second tower when it collapsed."
Thomas added, "I don't see myself as a hero. I just see myself as someone who wanted to give back."

A father of five, Thomas established Heroes Helping

Humanity in 2007. The non-profit organisation has a mission of improving the standard of living and quality of life for servicemen and women, and veterans and providing scholarships to economically-challenged students.

reddit referrer: Darrkman

Jim Lewis and Jim Springer

Reunited twins with incredible similarities

Jim Lewis and Jim Springer are twins who were separated three weeks after birth and adopted by different couples. Both couples (40 miles apart and unknown to each other) were told that their adoptive child had a twin who had died at birth. In February 1979, the twins suddenly rediscovered each other in Ohio, at age 39.

Upon meeting they soon realised their lives shared some extraordinary similarities.

Both couples had independently decided to name the boys James. Both married women named Linda, got divorced and remarried (both remarried women named Betty). One named his son James Alan, and the other named his son James Allan. Both had at one time owned dogs named Toy. Both men entered a form of law enforcement – one as a security guard, the other as a deputy sheriff. Both enjoyed woodworking, and the same brands of beer and tobacco. Both bit their nails.

Within two weeks of rediscovering each other, the twins were studied by Dr Thomas Bouchard at the University of Minnesota. Dr Bouchard was conducting a study on the effects of heredity and environment on human behaviour, and he jumped at the chance to study identical twins who had been separated since birth. Bouchard expected to find many differences between the twins, but instead discovered yet more striking similarities.

In one test which measured personality characteristics, the twins' scores were as close as the average of the totals of one person taking the test twice.

Brain wave tests produced remarkably similar profiles. Intelligence tests, mental abilities, gestures, voice tones, likes and dislikes were similar as well.

Both previously had high blood pressure and both had experienced what they thought were heart attacks. Both had undergone vasectomies. Both suffered from migraine headaches.

'The Jim Twins' were featured in a 1999 BBC documentary, Secret Life of Twins. Dr Bouchard commented that "the two twins are like a variation on a theme," with a greater than normal degree of shared characteristics, when compared with other identical twins.

reddit referrer: SoberAenima

Joan Ginther

The 'luckiest' woman in the world?

The chances of winning the lottery are pretty low. So, to win it four times? Impossible surely? Or incredibly lucky? Or indeed, was it luck at all?

Joan Ginther from Texas has won a multi-million-pound scratchcard lottery an incredible four times. But could this actually be down to her mathematical skills given that Joan is a professional statistician and a former maths professor? Unsurprisingly, Joan is remaining tight-lipped about her winning millions, and has now moved to Las Vegas.

The 63-year old American bought three of her winning scratchcards at a petrol station in the small border town of Bishop. Some locals have suggested that she had a deal with the owner of the store, to tip her off when a new shipment of high-stakes scratchcards came in. The owner would alert her and keep them aside for her to buy in bulk. Because, although the lottery companies would like us to believe that scratchcards are a random game, in fact they need to control the number of winners, and so each set of scratchcards printed contains a certain number of winning cards.

In the same way that those who regularly play in casinos might spot a pattern in cards dealt in blackjack, say (if there has been a slew of low-value cards, it means the next cards are more likely to be of high-value), you could possibly improve the odds in your favour of picking the winning scratchcard, by monitoring where previous winning tickets have come up – and when.

So was this Joan's method? Or was she just incredibly lucky? Well, she's not saying.

reddit referrer: Count_Bruno

Joseph Figlock, Cristina Torre and Mr Li

Babes in arms

Published in Time Magazine (October 17th, 1938) is the bizarre story of Joseph Figlock, a street sweeper who lived in Detroit, Michigan.

Figlock was cleaning a road one day when a baby fell from a fourth storey window, hitting him on the head and shoulders. Although both he and the baby were injured, the impact saved the baby's life.

The next year, while Figlock was cleaning another alley, a two year old named David Thomas fell from a window. Once again the baby was saved by landing on Figlock, and though presumably injured, both survived.

Figlock isn't around to save falling babies any more, but luckily others are.

In Brooklyn in 2013, a 16-month old baby boy named Dillon was spotted on a fire escape, apparently alone. A few passers-by climbed the fire escape to attempt to ensure his safety. Cristina Torre, who was at ground level at the time, later told The Guardian newspaper what happened next.

"Then he slipped. Instinctively, he grabbed on as he fell, so he was gripping the railing, hanging by his arms. I knew he couldn't hold on, 25 feet above the street, for long. I sensed people had gathered behind, but my attention was purely focused on my intention to catch the baby. I made sure I was positioned to save him.

"I told 911 he was falling and within a minute Dillon had. As he tumbled, he hit a protruding plastic sign for a yoga shop. There were shocked gasps as everyone heard his face knock the sign and he started to cry.

"I didn't move to catch him; I was in exactly the right spot. He just fell into my outstretched arms. He felt weightless. It was effortless. It felt like a basic and simple human response. Somehow I even managed to keep hold of my phone."

Luckily, baby Dillon suffered only a split lip.

And in May 2014, Mr Li, a street vendor in Zhongshan City, China, caught a baby who had fallen from a second-storey window during a thunderstorm. "I didn't think too much at the time. I was just afraid of failing to catch him," Mr Li told reporters. "It was nothing but human instinct to do so." The feat was captured on video (you can find it on YouTube).

reddit referrer: AbeltonSkive

Lara Lindstrom Clarke

Saved from 9/II by a chance encounter with Gwyneth Paltrow

On the morning of 11 September 2001, Lara Lindstrom Clarke was late for work. Rushing to catch her train, she ran out into the road in front of a Mercedes SUV. The driver of the SUV was Gwyneth Paltrow, returning home from an early yoga class. The two women stopped and waited for the other to proceed but without being able to communicate, the situation took a while to sort itself out.

Paltrow thought nothing more of the incident until she received a letter 10 years later from a woman called Lara Lindstrom Clarke. In her letter, Clarke explained how her chance encounter with Paltrow had made her miss the train to her workplace – the 77th floor of the South Tower of the World Trade Center. As a result, she arrived just as the first plane crashed into the North Tower and was able to escape unharmed. Four of Clarke's colleagues weren't so lucky, and although Clarke said, "At that time I was annoyed at everything that had made me late that day, including Gwyneth Paltrow", she thanked Paltrow in her letter for "changing [her] fate on that terrible day".

reddit referrer: sirmaxwell90

Martin van Butchell

An eccentric British dentist

A clause in a marriage contract reputedly led to an eccentric British dentist putting his dead wife on display because he would continue to receive income for only as long as she 'remained above ground'.

Martin van Butchell (1735-1814), famous in London for his extreme and outlandish behaviour, which included riding around Hyde Park on a white pony painted with purple or black spots, had trained under Dr William Turner, and turned to his tutor for help with embalming the body when his wife Mary died in 1775. Her body was injected with preservatives and colour additives, her eyes replaced with glass eyes, and she was placed in a glass-topped coffin.

The body was on display in the window of van Butchell's home, which also served as his practice, and drew many crowds. Some say the marriage clause reference was just a ruse to gain publicity and drum up customers for his dental work. Whatever the reason, it certainly drew attention to van Butchell and his work!

When he remarried, his second wife, Elizabeth, objected to the decomposing body, and it was given to John Hunter, brother of his old tutor William, for his museum collection. The body ended up in the Royal

College of Surgeons, and was finally destroyed by the
Germans in a bombing raid in 1941.

reddit referrer: AlDente

Nicolas Loufrani

Trademark owner of the lucrative 'smiley' face icon

The 'smiley face' icon is ubiquitous, with its circular yellow face and simple black smile. But did you know that it's also a trademarked symbol, and therefore its use must be licensed?

The most likely true originator of the smiley face was Harvey Ball, who in the early 1960s was a graphic designer working in Massachusetts, USA. Ball designed a yellow badge for a large assurance client, and was paid $45 for his efforts. However he didn't copyright the design.

During a legal battle with retail giant Walmart in 2006, Loufrani told the New York Times, "a prehistoric man probably invented the smiley face in some cave, but I certainly was the first to register it as a trademark". Loufrani's father, Franklin, had registered the design with French authorities in 1971 (incidentally the same year that Nicolas was born). The Walmart case was eventually settled before a US Federal court, although the settlement terms were not disclosed.

Starting in the 1990s, Nicolas developed the 'Smiley' brand, establishing the trademark and copyright in over 100 countries.

How ironic then, that a symbol of happiness has

caused so much controversy and legal strife. Perhaps to counter this negativity, Loufrani founded a charity, The SmileyWorld Association, selling ethical and fair trade products.

reddit referrer: marquis_of_chaos

Bando Mitsugoro VIII

Japanese actor who claimed to be able to survive the poison of the illegal Pufferfish

Bando Mitsugoro VIII was one of Japan's most celebrated actors in classical dance-drama, called Kabuki. His acting career started as a young boy of seven years old in 1913 but he really became famous in the 1930s and remained in the public eye until his death in 1975.

The most interesting thing about Mitsugoro's life however, was not his extensive acting career, but his death. In a Kyoto restaurant, where the actor had gone for an evening out with friends, he ordered four portions of the liver of the poisonous fish Fugu, or Pufferfish – *fugu kimo*. After claiming that he could survive the poison of the fish – the sale of which was prohibited – Mitsugoro ate all four portions of liver and returned to his hotel room.

Unfortunately, his boasts had apparently been based on machoism rather than any real tolerance and after an excruciating seven hours of paralysis and convulsions, Mitsugoro died.

reddit referrer: spellbreaker

Raffi Stepanian

New York City's gold and jewel miner

An unemployed diamond setter from Queens, Raffi Stepanian has found a novel way to use his skills – capitalising on the fragments of riches that have been lost in New York City over past decades.

After discovering small amounts gold on the floor of a New York diamond exchange, Raffi Stepanian reasoned that there must be gold lying outside too. Since this revelation, Stepanian has spent countless hours on his hands and knees, sifting through New York City's mud and sidewalk cracks armed only with his tweezers and backpack.

"The streets of 47th Street are literally paved with gold," Stepanian told the New York Post.

"The percentage of gold out here on the street is greater than the amount of gold you would find in a mine ... It comes close to a mother lode because in the street, you're picking up gold left by the industry."

He has sold most of his discoveries to metal refiners or diamond sellers, making around $500 per week.

"This is the gold that has been on this street for 60 years. I know how to look, and I know where to look for it."

reddit referrer: Ninjabackwards

Richard Parker

Shipwrecked, again

Anyone who has read Yann Martel's book *Life of Pi* (or seen the movie), will recognise the name 'Richard Parker' as the name of the Bengal tiger that is trying to eat the protagonist, a young boy, after both are shipwrecked and are forced to share a small life boat.

However, far fewer people are aware that 'Richard Parker' is the name of several real and fictional seamen who became shipwrecked, with some of them being cannibalised by their fellow shipmates.

In Edgar Allan Poe's only novel *The Narrative of Arthur Gordon Pym of Nantucket*, published in 1838, Richard Parker is a mutinous sailor on the whaling ship *Grampus*. After the ship capsizes in a storm, Parker suggests that he and three other survivors draw lots to kill one of them to sustain the others. Parker is the one who gets cannibalised.

In 1846 the *Francis Spaight* sailed into trouble at sea. Apprentice Richard Parker was among the 21 victims who drowned. And in 1884, the yacht *Mignonette* sank, leaving four survivors. They drifted in a lifeboat for days before one of them, the cabin boy, was eaten by the others. The cabin boy's name? Richard Parker.

reddit referrer: thebobstu

Roy Sullivan

The man who survived being hit by lightning more than any other, only to die of a broken heart

Four decades after he was added to the 'Guinness Book of World Records', US Park Ranger Roy Sullivan continues to hold the dubious distinction of being struck by lightning more than any known person.

Between 1942 and his death in 1983, Sullivan was struck by lightning seven times.

The first lightning strike burned a half-inch strip all along his right leg and knocked his big toenail off. In 1969, a second strike burned off his eyebrows and knocked him unconscious. Another strike, while in his front yard just a year later, left his shoulder seared.

In 1972 Sullivan was working inside a ranger station in Shenandoah National Park when he was hit again – his hair was set on fire. Perhaps not surprisingly, at this point Sullivan developed a fear of death, and specifically of being struck again. Sullivan would do what he could to avoid lightning, but being a park ranger in an area with frequent lightning during summer months put him at higher risk than most. As it turned out, he was right to be worried.

In 1973 while he was out on patrol in the park, Sullivan saw a storm cloud forming and drove away quickly. But the cloud, he said later, seemed to be following him. When he finally thought he had outrun it, he decided it was safe to leave his truck. Soon after, he was struck by a lightning bolt. The lightning set his hair on fire (again), moved down his left arm and left leg and knocked off his shoe. It then crossed over to his right leg just below the knee. Still conscious, Sullivan crawled to his truck and poured the can of water, which he always kept there (at least he was prepared by now), over his head.

A sixth strike in 1976 left him with an injured ankle. The last lightning bolt to hit Roy Sullivan occurred whilst fishing in 1977, and left him with a burnt stomach and yet more singed hair. As if that weren't bad enough, immediately after the strike, a bear tried to steal trout from his fishing line. Sullivan hit the bear with a tree branch. He claimed that this was the 22nd time he had hit a bear with a stick in his lifetime. Yet another peril of being a park ranger.

All seven lightning strikes were documented by the superintendent of Shenandoah National Park, R Taylor Hoskins, and were verified by doctors.

Later in life Sullivan was avoided by people due to their fear of being hit by lightning, and this saddened him. He once recalled: "For instance, I was walking with the Chief Ranger one day when lightning struck way off.

The Chief said, 'I'll see you later'."

Sullivan recalled that the first time he was struck by lightning was not in 1942 but much earlier. When he was a child, he was helping his father to cut wheat in a field, when a thunderbolt struck the blade of his scythe without injuring him. But because he could not prove the incident, he never claimed it.

Sadly, despite surviving lightning so many times, in 1983 at the age of 71, Sullivan took his own life, apparently over an unrequited love.

Roy Sullivan still holds the record for the person struck by lightning more recorded times than any other human being. One of his ranger hats is on display at the Guinness World Exhibit, showing two scorched holes where a lightning bolt entered and exited.

reddit referrer: liverman

Sam Eisho

Businessman and former refugee tried to repay over $18,000 in welfare money

In the late 1990s, Sam Eisho was apprehended at an Iraqi checkpoint whilst attempting to reach his native Kurdistan, northern Iraq. Locked in a cell, Eisho narrowly avoided being tortured and killed by Iraqi guards – thanks to a chance encounter with a soldier whom he knew from university. Eisho pleaded for his life and was freed.

Not long afterwards, Eisho and his wife decided to escape Iraq, and after declaring asylum in Greece, they worked in a mattress factory for four years whilst waiting for a visa to Australia. In 1999 they secured the visa – thanks to Eisho's uncle, a doctor already living there.

Over the years Eisho was given state aid as he worked his way up, culminating in running his own successful construction business. So, in 2007, after calculating the amount he had received over the years from the Australian government, Eisho went to a local Centrelink (the Australian welfare/benefits centre) with a cheque for $18,681.43.

"They said 'the line is there' and I said 'no, I'm here to pay you'," Eisho said.

Eisho's cheque was returned to him, with the suggestion that he donated the money – which he did. Eisho has also, he said, donated around $60,000 to hospitals, and his daughter's primary school.

"Eventually, due to the great opportunities in this land, I was able to find work, and then after some time, set up my own business," said Eisho when speaking to Sydney's *Daily Telegraph* newspaper in 2013.

"My appreciation for the opportunities of this country are always on my lips. I always feel deep within me the need to repay the money that I received."

"I feel good when I have paid back someone. Then I go to bed and the pillow is just fantastic. This is the big secret in life – treat others the way you want to be treated," he said.

reddit referrer: michaeldunworthsydne

Saroo Munshi Khan

Finding his way home using Google Earth

Saroo Munshi Khan was just five years old when he became separated from his family, and it was not until he was 31 that he finally saw them again, with the help of Google Earth.

In 1986, Saroo had been collecting coins on trains with his older brother, and had fallen asleep on the platform whilst his brother continued looking for money. When Saroo awoke, his brother was nowhere to be seen, and so he boarded the nearest train. However, instead of taking him home to Khandwa it took him to Calcutta. Alone in an unknown city, Saroo lived on the streets for a time, before being found and taken to an orphanage. From there, he was adopted by an Australian family, and moved to live in Tasmania. Saroo never fully forgot his Indian family though, and always dreamed of finding them again someday.

More than 20 years later, having graduated from college, Saroo became obsessed with the idea of finding his family again, and spent hours at a time on Google Earth, attempting to find his village.

Using his mathematical knowledge, Saroo worked out how far his train was likely to have gone from the local station to Calcutta, given train speeds and time.

From this information, he had a radius to work within. The areas within the radius which didn't speak Hindi, or had cold climates were discounted, further narrowing the search. After many more hours of searching, Saroo chanced upon a familiar landmark – a bridge next to a train station. From here, he could easily scroll the way back to his neighbourhood.

In 2012, Saroo finally boarded a plane that took him to India, and a series of trains which took him to Khandwa. From there, he remembered the walk to his home. Whilst his family had moved house since, they were easily found, and, 26 years after their accidental separation, Saroo was reunited with his mother, sister and remaining brother. Saroo's mother, Fatima, describes how "the happiness in my heart was as deep as the sea" as a result of this miraculous reunion.

reddit referrer: Aboly

Steve Flaig

Searching for his birth mother for four years – found she works at same store

For Michigan delivery truck-driver Steve Flaig, adopted at birth, his search for his birth mother ended up being rather close to home – she turned out to be his co-worker.

Flaig decided to look for his birth mother on turning 18, with the support of his adopted parents. The adoption agency provided the paperwork and he began his search on the internet – but came up with nothing.

Four years later, when he looked at the paperwork again, he realised he'd been spelling his mother's surname incorrectly – he had typed in Talladay, instead of Tallady. This time he got a result for the name of someone who lived less than a mile away from Lowe's store in Grand Rapids where he worked.

He happened to mention this to his boss, who replied: "You mean Chris Tallady, who works here?"

Chris Tallady had started work at the store about eight months earlier, as head cashier, whilst Steve Flaig had been working there for two years.

It was a very emotional reunion when both realised their relationship went beyond being co-workers. Sometimes what you seek really is very close to home.

reddit user: user's account no longer active

Tom Attridge

Pilot who shot down his own plane

During the 1950s, jet aircraft technology was improving at a rapid pace. Records were regularly broken, and new prototypes were constantly being developed and tested.

So it was in 1956 that 33-year-old former Navy pilot Tom Attridge found himself flying a test aircraft over the Atlantic Ocean, for the Grumman Aircraft Engineering Corporation. His supersonic F11F 'Tiger' aircraft had been modified for manoeuvrability and naval use.

Attridge's task that day was to test fire the Tiger's 20mm canon. Two miles from base, he entered a shallow dive at 13,000 feet and fired a short burst of around 70 rounds. Powering the afterburners, he accelerated into a steep dive and fired the cannons again.

A few seconds later the windshield received an impact, which he thought to have been a bird – a not-uncommon occurrence when flying over coastlines. One engine started to suffer too, which Attridge described as sounding "like it was tearing up".

He headed for base, but the engines began to cut out, and he realised his aircraft wasn't going to make it back. Attridge's Tiger crash-landed into woods, just half a mile from the runway. His plane careered through 300 feet of trees, the right wing was torn off, flames appeared as fuel caught fire and ammunition started firing. Although injured with broken vertebrae and a broken leg, father of three Attridge was hospitalised and survived.

An investigation into the crash revealed its cause – and it wasn't a bird. During the afterburner dive, Attridge had accelerated into the path of his own bullets. One went through the windshield, another hit the plane's nose cone and a third struck the right engine. Fortunately the plane was not equipped that day with combat-standard, explosive shells, otherwise the outcome would have been far worse.

The bullets' speed at the moment of firing was calculated at 4,300 feet per second (the muzzle velocity plus the airplane's speed), but due to air friction and gravity they slowed considerably and began to fall. Diving at an estimated 880 miles an hour, Attridge's plane caught up with the bullets at the exact point where the trajectories of the bullets and the plane intersected, 11 seconds after firing. By this point the plane was travelling much faster than the bullets, and the result was effectively the reverse of a gunshot – the 'target' hit the bullets.

Following this incident, the US Navy instructed jet pilots of to turn off course or pull up after firing their guns. "At the speeds we're flying today, it could be duplicated any time," Attridge warned.

Just six months later Attridge was back flying again. He continued his career with Grumman, working on the first lunar module, used for the Apollo 9 mission. He later became vice president of Grumman Ecosystems.

reddit referrer: tomega

William Horace de Vere Cole

Legendary prankster

William Horace de Vere Cole was the quintessential, upper-class, practical joker. Born into a wealthy Anglo-Irish family in 1881, Cole was educated at Eton and then Trinity College.

Whilst at Cambridge University, Cole began his hoaxing. When he learned that the Sultan of Zanzibar was visiting Britain, Cole telegrammed his university college to inform them that the Sultan was planning a visit. Dressed in Arabian-style attire, Cole proceeded to visit his own college impersonating a translator to the 'Sultan' – who was actually his friend Adrian Stephen. The men were treated to a grand tour of the city and university. The hoax was later revealed when it was discovered that the real Sultan had been in London at the time but, to avoid any recriminations, Cole and his friends kept quiet until after they'd left college.

Raising the stakes in 1910, Cole pretended to be a Foreign Office official, and sent a message to the HMS *Dreadnought* in Weymouth, that the Emperor of Abyssinia was scheduled to visit for a tour of the ship. The 'Emperor' visited, accompanied by an entourage including Adrian Stephen (this time he was the translator), and Stephen's sister – who would later become famous as Virginia Woolf.

The British Royal Navy fell for it, giving their distinguished guests the full VIP treatment, including a guard of honour, a full tour of the ship and its famous guns.

With blackened faces, and dressed in costumes and wigs, Cole and his chums spoke in a nonsense language which led to the hoax later being referred to as the 'Bunga-Bunga Affair'. Cole told the press the truth a few days later, bringing embarrassment to the Navy. 'Bunga! Bunga!' became a music hall joke, and when the real Emperor of Abyssinia arrived in Britain not long afterwards, even he was subjected to the chant.

Whilst the *Dreadnought* hoax was most likely a simple 'jape', commentators have remarked that it revealed much. Historian Gilbert Highet wrote that the incident "exposed the uncritical readiness of the British government and of the Royal Navy ... the silly little blackface impersonation by half a dozen unemployed youngsters proved to be a satire on the entire British imperial system".

Cole and his pals managed to concoct many other pranks.

On one occasion, Cole dared an old schoolfriend from Eton, and Member of Parliament, Oliver Locker-Lampson, to a race along a London street. Cole gave his friend a head start — having already slipped his gold watch into the MP's pocket. As soon as Locker-Lampson began to run, Cole yelled "Stop thief!" and a nearby policeman apprehended the MP. Despite convincing the policeman of their innocence, Cole managed to cause further disruption, resulting in both men being arrested.

In another cheeky stunt, Cole bought every ticket in the stalls at a play he thought was terrible, and gave the tickets to many of his well-to-do acquaintances. Once the house lights were raised, the audience members in the higher levels erupted with gasps and laughter, and the show was halted. Cole had surreptitiously positioned bald men in the stalls so that the formation of their heads would together spell out a profanity.

Ever the mischief-maker, Cole took advantage of his physical likeness to British prime minister Ramsay MacDonald by impersonating him, giving speeches that contradicted MacDonald's political views and criticized the Labour Party.

According to legend, guests at one of Cole's parties discovered that they all had the word 'bottom' in their surnames. He was also a suspect in the Piltdown Man hoax.

The Time-Life *Library of Curious and Unusual Facts* described that:

"Cole often targeted his peers. For example, playing on the innate good manners of the well-bred English gent, Cole would pose as a surveyor on the street and politely ask a passing swell to help by holding one end of a string for a moment. Then the prankster would disappear around the corner, find another man to hold the other end of the string, and walk away.

"He was also fond of spontaneous pranks. When he stumbled on a road crew without a foreman one day, Cole leaped into the breach and directed the men to London's busy Piccadilly Circus, where he had them excavate a huge trench in the street. A nearby policeman obligingly redirected the heavy downtown traffic all day, and it was several hours before the city noticed the unauthorized hole."

In April 1919, Cole was honeymooning in Venice. Unfortunately he couldn't help himself but leave his new wife for a night for a quick trip to the mainland. The next day was April Fool's Day, and Cole had fetched horse manure and distributed it in the Piazza di San Marco, which caused much confusion for the residents as Venice – a city with no horses. We're not sure what his wife thought of this, however.

Cole died in poverty, in France in 1936. The following year, his brother-in-law became Prime Minister.

reddit referrer: TeleSavalas

CRIME

"You can get much farther with a kind word and a gun than you can with a kind word alone."

– Al Capone

Andre Bamberski

Father who arranged the kidnapping of his daughter's killer

In 1982, Frenchman Andre Bamberski's daughter Kalinka was spending a summer holiday in Bavaria with her mother and stepfather. During the holiday 14-year-old Kalinka died in suspicious circumstances. Bamberski was to spend the next three decades fighting for justice.

Autopsy results showed that Kalinka had been given a cobalt-based injection shortly before her death. Bamberski urged German authorities to investigate Kalinka's stepfather, Dieter Krombach, a German doctor. Bamberski suspected that Krombach had injected Kalinka so he could rape her, and that the drug had caused her death.

Krombach admitted giving Kalinka injections. At first he claimed it was intended to aid in tanning; later he said it was intended to treat anaemia. He also claimed to have administered various injections intended to revive Kalinka before calling the emergency services. He later said that he had also given her a sleeping pill that night.

Bamberski spent years battling with police, prosecutors and the European Court of Justice in a bid to get Krombach extradited from Germany to France and face trial. German prosecutors had dropped the case against Krombach, deciding the death was accidental.

In France in 1995 Krombach was convicted in absentia of manslaughter and sentenced to 15 years in jail. But the verdict was annulled in 2001 by the European Court of Human Rights because Krombach had not been able to defend himself. As a result, Krombach received compensation of 100,000 francs.

In a separate incident in 1997, Krombach pleaded guilty in Germany to raping a 16-year-old girl after sedating her in his office. He was given a two-year suspended sentence and banned from practising. Later he was jailed for 28 months for practising medicine without a licence.

In 2004 a German court again declined the French authorities' extradition request of Krombach, stating that the case was closed.

Concerned that the statute of limitations would soon run out, Bamberksi decided to take justice into his own hands. In 2009 he hired Russian kidnappers to abduct Krombach, then aged 74, from Germany and take him across the border into France.

In October that year, Krombach was found, bound and bleeding, chained to a fence outside the prosecutor's office in Mulhouse, a French city close to the German border.

Despite Germany's demands for Krombach's return,

a new trial was convened. Several women testified at the trial that Krombach had sexually abused them as teenagers, always involving cobalt-iron injections. Kalinka's mother, Danielle Gonnin, told the court that she had found Kalinka lifeless in bed, and said: "I immediately thought of the injection, but Dieter Krombach told me, 'No, there's never been any problem with these injections'."

In 2011, nearly 30 years after Kalinka's death, Krombach was sentenced to 15 years in prison, for causing intentional bodily harm resulting in unintentional death. Krombach later appealed, and lost.

Speaking to the Daily Telegraph, Bamberski told of his delight with the verdict:

"My first thought is for Kalinka," he said. "What I promised her, what I wanted was a complete and fair trial. Now that goal has been reached. Justice has been done in her memory and now I will be able to mourn for her."

In 2014, Bamberski, then 76, stood trial himself in eastern France and was convicted of ordering a cross-border kidnapping. He was given a one-year suspended prison sentence. Two other men were convicted of carrying out the kidnapping. Each was sentenced to one year in prison.

reddit referrer: Kamon2011

Anonymous Robber

Almost 300 million yen was stolen from a Japanese bank, and the robber was never found

On 10th December 1968, 294,307,500 yen was being transported by four employees of the Kokobunji branch of the Nihon Shintaku Ginko, Toshiba's Fuchu Factory, where it would be used to pay bonuses to employees. The boxes containing the money were in metal boxes in a company car, and they had travelled just 400m away from the bank when a policeman on a motorbike stopped them on the road next to the Toyko Fuchu Prison. The officer warned that there might be dynamite in the company car, as their manager's house had been blown up. This claim was plausible because the bank manager had been receiving threatening letters at the time.

All four Kokobunji employees left the vehicle, and the police officer crawled under the car in an attempt to find out whether there was any dynamite there. Flames and smoke appeared, and the police officer shouted that it was going to explode. Although it was only a warning flare under the car, the employees had no way of knowing this, and panicked, running from the car to the prison walls. This enabled the police officer to get into the car and drive it away.

Nearly fifty years later, there is still no knowledge about who committed the theft, despite an investigation involving hundreds of police and costing more than 12 million US dollars. The police motorbike left at the scene was discovered to be a fake painted to look like a real one. More than 100 other pieces of evidence were left at the scene, which were mostly every day objects that had been scattered to cause confusion. There were a few suspects during the course of the investigation, but there was not sufficient evidence to conclusively prove it was any one of them.

The statute of limitations on the crime has long since expired, meaning the thief will not face punishment for his actions, should he ever be discovered.

reddit referrer: TheCannon

John Morales – McGruff the Crime Dog

Famous for crime prevention campaigns, he became a criminal himself

'McGruff the Crime Dog', famous in the US for his efforts to prevent crime, was sentenced to 16 years in prison.

McGruff is a cartoon character of a bloodhound dog, with the slogan: 'taking a bite out of crime'. He has been used in the US since 1980 for educational purposes, in order to build up crime awareness in children, through educational booklets and short films. McGruff is commonly used as a puppet, and police have also dressed up as him in order to aid his campaign, which raises awareness of issues such as drugs and safety.

One of the actors who has played the part of McGruff is John Morales, who dressed up as the dog for the Harris County Sherriff's Association in the 1990s. However, John did not heed the advice that the character he was playing gave, as he was given a sentence of 16 years in prison in 2011. Having been pulled over by the police for speeding, the Crime Dog was discovered to have marijuana seeds in the boot of his car, and diagrams for indoor pot growing systems on the front seat. Authorities then searched his house, and found more than one thousand marijuana plants growing there. They also discovered nine thousand rounds of ammunition and 27 weapons, which included shotguns, rifles and a grenade launcher. John claimed that the only reason he grew the marijuana was to earn money to help sick relatives.

The 41 year old pleaded guilty to the crimes, and was sentenced to sixteen years in a federal prison. He insisted that he wasn't a violent person, but the judge responded: 'Everything I read about you makes you seem like a scary person."

Possession of weapons and drugs shows that McGruff the Crime Dog obviously did not practise what he preached.

reddit referrer: rino23

McArthur Wheeler

What a lemon

In 1995, 44 year old Wheeler robbed two banks in one day. He brazenly walked in, committed the robberies, and walked out again, all the time appearing to make no attempt to hide his actions.

However, this normal-looking man was wearing what he thought was a cleverly thought-out disguise. Wheeler was aware that lemon juice has some unusual properties. An example of this is writing with lemon juice, which cannot be seen until it is heated. Based on this knowledge, Wheeler believed that if he put lemon juice all over his face, his face would not be visible, so he wouldn't be caught on security cameras.

He had tested this theory out by covering his face in lemon juice prior to the day of the burglary, and taking a photo of himself with a polaroid camera. This produced a blank image, which he took to be proof that the disguise would work.

The images taken from the security cameras at the banks during the robbery were played on the evening news that night though, and Wheeler was quickly recognised and arrested.

Psychologists have found this case to be of much interest, due to how it shows that the less competent an individual is at a task, the more likely they are to inflate their self-appraised competence in relationship to that task. This has come to be known as The Dunning and Kuger effect, named after researchers who were inspired by the case of McArthur Wheeler.

This competence effect is proved by Wheeler's genuine shock at being caught on camera. Whilst in police custody, Wheeler was shown the images of the robbery and is reported to have commented: "But I wore the juice!"

reddit referrer: YesIAmYou

Michael Malloy

Survived numerous attempts on his life by acquaintances trying to claim life insurance

An alcoholic and homeless in New York, Michael Malloy seemed to be the man who refused to die. Five men who were acquainted with him – Tony Marino, Joseph Murphy, Francis Pasqua, Hershey Green and Daniel Kriesberg – decided to commit life insurance fraud, by taking out three policies on Malloy, and then get him to drink himself to death.

This was at the start of 1933, before Prohibition was relaxed, and Marino ran a 'speakeasy' – an establishment that sold illegal liquor. Initially Malloy was given unlimited credit there, but although he drank for most of the waking day, it did not kill him. The plotters then tried substituting antifreeze, but Malloy would just drink until he passed out, then come back for more the next day.

After that ploy failed, the gang tried turpentine, followed by horse liniment, and then finally mixing in rat poison. To no avail: Malloy came back for more.

Having decided that they couldn't kill him through any form of drink – or food: they also tried oysters soaked in wood alcohol – the gang now attempted to freeze him to death. Picking a cold night, they took the passed-out Malloy to a park, dumped him in the snow and poured gallons of water on his chest. Yet the next day Malloy was back at the speakeasy.

Next, they tried to run him over – Green's taxi hit him at 45 mph – and this hospitalised him for three weeks with broken bones. But he was soon back at the bar.

The gang settled on one last attempt. Again, waiting until he had passed out, they put a hose in Malloy's mouth and turned on the gas. This time he was dead within the hour and the gang were able to claim their money.

The five men made the mistake of boasting about their fraud, and squabbling over the spoils which led the police to take an interest, and they had Malloy's body exhumed and examined. After a trial, all five men were found guilty, with Green being sent to prison and the other four executed by electric chair.

Michael Malloy's numerous brushes with death have been immortalised in popular culture including songs written about him, plays based on his life, and he has also featured in television programmes.

reddit referrer: segaliberationarmy

Pedro López, 'Monster of the Andes'

Colombian serial killer who murdered more than 300 young girls in South America and was released from jail after only 14 years

After a troubled childhood, Pedro López, widely known in South America as 'Monster of the Andes' was first put behind bars for car theft in 1969, an ordeal which rendered him almost insane.

On his release, López roamed around Peru, preying on girls from local tribes. By 1978 when he was 29 years old, López claimed that he had already killed more than 100 girls and was on the point of being executed by a Peruvian tribe when an American missionary intervened and handed him over to the police who promptly released him without punishment.

Having escaped punishment from both tribesmen and the police, López claimed that over the next two years he killed girls in Ecuador and Colombia at a horrifying rate of three girls a week. Finally, in 1980, the vicious murderer was cornered and held down by local market traders and arrested by police. He confessed to the murders of more than 300 young girls, a statement which was regarded as untrue until a mass grave was uncovered by flash flooding.

For his crimes he was sentenced to just 16 years in an Ecuadorian prison and was released two years early, apparently due to good behaviour. This brought his sentence to a mere 14 years, only double the amount of time he was jailed for car theft.

reddit referrer: IAMAnarcissist

Susan Walters

Strangled the hitman her husband sent to murder her

In 2006, nurse Susan Walters returned as usual from work to her home in Portland, Oregon. But on this day she soon found herself fighting for her life.

Lying in wait was an intruder wielding a hammer, which he used to repeatedly hit Walters on the head. After about 15 minutes of intense fighting, and suffering multiple injuries, Walters managed to subdue the intruder in a choke hold. She tried to find out who had sent him. But the man resumed his attack, so Walters, fearing for her life, again strangled him – ultimately killing him.

The intruder was Edward Haffey, a crack addict and convicted criminal. Notes in Haffey's backpack linked him to Walters' estranged husband, Michael Kuhnhausen. Police discovered that Kuhnhausen had paid Haffey $50,000 to murder his wife of 17 years, and make it seem like a robbery 'gone wrong'.

Kuhnhausen pleaded guilty, receiving 10 years as part of a plea deal. With good behaviour this was reduced to eight years, and in September 2014 he was released.

Walters survived her attack, lucky to be alive. But she was left with anxieties about her ex-husband's release from prison. She bought a new home, with an alarm system and security cameras. She also devised a plan so she can go into hiding at a moment's notice.

Prior to Kuhnhausen's release, Walters spoke to The Oregonian newspaper of her continuing fears: "It's disturbing that he's getting out, but I know I can't keep him there.

"I'm hoping he hasn't found someone in prison who said, 'You just hired the wrong guy'."

Walters has help from a team of criminal justice professionals, and is appealing to the Oregon Board of Parole and Post-Prison Supervision to ban Kuhnhausen from entering the county in which she lives.

"I was forced to kill another man," Walters said. "Even though he was not a good man, that was the hardest part."

Susan Walters was awarded the Civilian Medal of Heroism by the Portland Police Bureau.

reddit user: user's account no longer active

The 'Chiasso' financial smugglers

The world's largest ever smuggling seizure?

We'd like to tell you their names, but we can't. In fact, there are a quite a few mysteries associated with these individuals.

Here's what we can tell you. On 3 June 2009, in the Swiss town of Chiasso, close to the Italian border, two ordinary-looking, Japanese men in their mid-50s were stopped by customs officials. Hiding below a false bottom inside the men's suitcases were US Treasury bonds, totalling an incredible $134.5 billion (more than the GDP of New Zealand).

A commander of the financial police in Como stated that the bonds were "made of filigree paper of excellent quality" and the two men had bank paperwork that supported their provenance. The bonds were also in very high denominations, only available to nation states. Commentators speculated whether the bonds were in fact genuine, and – given the extraordinarily large sums involved – what the effect might be on levels of confidence in the US dollar and general international finance.

What happened next is far from clear. The Financial Times reported that the two men had been released, but were not named and no reason for release was given. Japanese authorities expressed interest in the incident, but were not told about their release or their whereabouts.

Italian law claims 40% of any undeclared currency brought across their borders over the value of €10,000. If the bonds were declared genuine, Italy could have claimed a huge €38 billion from the US. So you won't be surprised to learn that the US Secret Service became involved, declaring that the bonds were fakes, probably the work of the mafia.

If the bonds had been considered genuine, these two Japanese men would have been the US' fourth largest creditor (behind Russia) as well as perpetrators of the largest single smuggling incident ever known.

reddit referrer: axolotl_peyotl

William Harrison

Three hanged for murder of a man who reappeared after being missing for two years

William Harrison disappeared on 16th August 1660. He was an estate manager from the town of Chipping Campden, in Gloucestershire, and left his home to walk to the nearby village of Charingworth in order to visit a tenant. When he did not return, his servant, John Perry, and later, his son, Edward Harrison, were sent to look for him. The pair could not find him, but heard from the tenant he had visited that Harrison had been seen the night before, on his way back home. As there was no more news of him, Perry and Edward Harrison returned to Chipping Campden.

However, on their way home, the pair heard that William Harrison's hat, shirt and collar had been discovered on the road. Although the hat bore marks of being slashed with a sharp implement, and the shirt and collar were stained with blood, there was no body.

On returning home, there was no further news of William's fate, although the townsfolk were beginning to suspect that Perry had killed his master in order to take his money. John Perry was questioned, and confessed he knew William to be murdered, though he pleaded not guilty to having caused this. Instead, he claimed his mother, Joan, and brother, Richard, had killed William. There was basis for this claim because they had previously stolen money from William Harrison's house.

All three were found guilty of the murder of William Harrison, and sentenced to death by hanging. Joan was executed first, as she was believed to be a witch who had cast a spell on her sons to make them carry out the murder.

Two years after this, William Harrison arrived back in England, off a ship from Lisbon. He claimed that he had been abducted by pirates, and sold into slavery in Turkey. After his master's death, he had escaped and paid passage to Dover using a silver bowl he had been given. Whilst it cannot be proved if this was the truth, his return did prove nevertheless the innocence of all three Perrys.

reddit referrer: Ninja_OT

POLITICS

*"Too bad that all the people who know how to run the
country are busy driving taxicabs and cutting hair."*

– George Burns

Harold Holt

Australian prime minister who went for a swim and disappeared

Despite being Prime Minister of Australia, and a leading politician for many years before that, Harold Holt is most remembered for the manner of his death. He had been prime minister for 22 months, when he went for a swim off the Victorian coast – and never returned.

Holt had driven from Melbourne down Port Philip Bay on 17 December 1967 with three friends and his two bodyguards, and despite heavy surf decided to go for a swim at Point Nepean. The spot is famous for its strong currents and dangerous riptides, and his friends tried to discourage Holt from swimming. He soon disappeared from view and his friends raised the alarm. Soon after a full search operation was underway, including divers from the Royal Australian Navy, RAAF helicopters and local volunteers. But no trace of Holt was found.

Holt was a strong swimmer, but had been suffering ill health, and had been told by his doctor to desist from swimming whilst a shoulder injury healed.

Because his body was never found, it fuelled the rumour mill and gave rise to many urban myths, with speculation that he had committed suicide; that he'd been kidnapped by a Chinese submarine; or that he'd been abducted by a UFO.

No inquest was held at the time but Victorian law was changed in 1985 and old cases were re-opened, and in 2005 the Coroner found that Holt had drowned in accidental circumstances.

Perhaps to ensure that Holt is most remembered for his watery end, rather than his political achievements in his 32 years in Parliament, he is commemorated by the Harold Holt Swim Centre in Melbourne. The complex was under construction at the time of his death, and was named after him as the suburb's local member.

reddit referrer: Lonzy

Craig Monteilh

FBI undercover agent reported for acting suspiciously

Craig Monteilh was reported to the FBI on suspicion of being a dangerous religious extremist. However, the Orange County Muslim community who reported him did not realise that Monteilh was actually working undercover for the FBI at the time.

Monteilh chanced upon conversation with off-duty police whilst at the gym, where he mentioned the criminal fraud of his past, which had resulted in a prison sentence. The abundance of information about criminals that Monteilh had picked up whilst in prison suggested to the police that he would be useful in undercover work. They soon assigned him work on organised crime cases before later suggesting he worked with anti-terrorism.

Under the alias of Farouk Aziz, 49 year old Monteilh was to spend time in mosques and with local Islamic communities, in order to record conversations and find out if there were any radical threats. Monteilh began by simply spending time in mosques, praying and reading, under the pretence of having a genuine interest in the religion. The purpose of this was for conversations to begin, and friendships to be formed, so Monteilh was not seen as a suspicious figure.

Over time, he grew a beard and began to wear

robes, and then the instructions came from the FBI to start questioning those around him. Using recording devices on his keyring or in his clothing, Monteilh posed deliberate leading questions to those around him. He made every effort to have these conversations with as many people as possible, even going to the extremes of seducing Muslim women to gain further chances to record conversation. These included talking of injustices towards Muslims, American foreign policy, and the desire to become a martyr. All these intended to elicit a response of agreement, which would then be followed up.

The FBI's aims were two-fold: they wanted to prevent any possible threat from radical extremists, but also wanted to discover who may have been put in a difficult position by the Muslim community, for example due to homosexuality or adultery. These people could be targeted as future possible undercover agents, as they were already within the Muslim community, so could easily access information.

However, the local Muslim communities felt such unease at Monteilh's questions that they reported him to the FBI as an extremist, and the Islamic Centre of Irvine had a restraining order placed on him. This meant the life of Farouk Aziz could no longer go on, and the undercover mission was over.

reddit referrer: blackstar9000

Frank Wills

His discovery at the Watergate Complex led to the resignation of President Nixon, but he was rendered almost unemployable and died destitute

After several years struggling with unemployment in Washington due to the race riots, in 1972 Frank finally secured a minimum wage job as a security guard. The job was at the Watergate complex, where the Democratic National Committee had their headquarters. The ease of the job was emphasised as the security guards were only expected to carry a can of mace, and there had only been one attempted break in that year.

Frank began work at midnight as usual on Saturday 17th June, and made his normal way round the offices on each floor, checking every individual door handle. However, he noticed the catch of a basement door fastened back with duct tape on his first round. Unsuspecting, he assumed it was an engineer carrying out work, as this often happened at night times, and they needed to be able to get back into the room easily. Frank removed the duct tape, and thought nothing more of it. When he returned to check the door again, he found it taped up again in the same manner as on the first time round. Alarmed at this, he immediately phoned for the Second Precinct Police. James McCord and four companions were found in the offices, and the following trial resulted in the Watergate Scandal.

Frank Wills was given an award for his 'unique role in the history of the nation', and used his new fame to try and improve the quality of life for himself and his fellow security workers, but to no avail. After this, Frank found it increasingly difficult to find work, possibly due to his rise in fame. He comments on the incident that "I put my life on the line. I went out of my way. If it wasn't for me, Woodward and Bernstein would not have known anything about Watergate".

reddit referrer: 3ofspades

Jean-Bédel Bokassa

'Cannibal' dictator

Dictators such as Idi Amin and Pol Pot are infamous for their cruel treatment of their own citizens. One lesser-known, but equally frightening dictator was Jean-Bédel Bokassa, one-time ruler of the Central African Republic.

Born in French Equatorial Africa, Bokassa joined the French colonial army in 1939, winning medals and rising to the rank of captain. In 1960, French Equatorial Africa became independent and was renamed as the Central African Republic. The new president David Dacko, who was his distant cousin, invited Bokassa to head the armed forces.

In 1966 Bokassa instigated a coup to oust Dacko, and declared himself President. He then began a reign of terror.

Taking all important government posts for himself, Bokassa personally supervised judicial beatings and introduced a rule that thieves would have an ear cut off for the first two offences and a hand for the third.

In 1977, in emulation of his hero Napoleon, he renamed the Central African Republic the Central African Empire and crowned himself emperor. The ceremony cost $20 million, which practically bankrupted the country. His diamond-encrusted crown alone cost $5 million.

In 1979 he had hundreds of schoolchildren arrested for refusing to wear uniforms made in a factory he owned, and was reported to have personally supervised the massacre of 100 of the schoolchildren by his Imperial Guard.

Bokassa's brutal 14-year rule ended in 1979 when French paratroopers overthrew his Government while Mr Bokassa was on an official trip to Libya. The country reverted to its former name as the Central African Republic. In his absence, he was tried and sentenced to death. Bokassa was immediately arrested by the Central African authorities as soon as he stepped off the plane and was tried for 14 different charges, including treason, murder and cannibalism.

Incredibly, at the time cannibalism was classed as a misdemeanour, so Bokassa could not be punished, even if he was found guilty. Nevertheless, former president Dacko testified that, immediately after the 1979 coup, he had seen photographs of bodies hanging in the cold-storage rooms of Bokassa's palace. When the defence argued that the photographs did not prove the bodies were for human consumption, Bokassa's former security chief of the palace was called to testify that he had cooked human flesh stored in the walk-in freezers and served it to Bokassa. Rumours circulated that Bokassa had served human flesh to French President Giscard d'Estaing, but this was not covered in the trial.

Throughout the trial, Bokassa denied all the charges against him. He was cleared of cannibalism but found guilty of other crimes, including the murder of schoolchildren. His death sentence was subsequently reduced to life in solitary confinement. But just six years later, in 1993, he was freed.

Unlike other former dictators who are often forced to live in exile, Bokassa lived the rest of his days in Bangui, the city which had been his capital. He died of a heart attack in 1996, aged 75.

reddit referrer: IoCarry

Prince Henry (Heinrich) of Prussia

King of America?

Americans are typically proud of their republic. But it nearly wasn't a republic at all. For a brief moment early in US history, the idea of a king was proposed.

In 1786 the young United States, and its standing in the world, was in flux.

Either Nathaniel Gorham, then-President of the Continental Congress, or Friedrich Wilhelm von Steuben, the Prussian general who served in the Continental Army, approached Alexander Hamilton with an idea.

Hamilton, a founding father of the United States and chief staff aide to General George Washington, was known to be favourably inclined toward monarchy. With this in mind, Gorham and von Steuben suggested to him that Prince Henry of Prussia – the younger brother of the famous Prussian warrior-king Frederick the Great – might become President, or even King, of the United States.

This was just a year before the US Constitution was created. Prussia had been one of the first European nations to recognize the USA and the two countries were on good terms.

Before Henry could respond, however, the conspirators change their minds and revoked their offer.

Hamilton became one of the most influential interpreters and promoters of the US Constitution

History may have played out very differently had the offer been open long enough for Prince Henry to accept.

reddit referrer: Wrestlingisgood

Sampat Pal Devi

Indian campaigner for women's rights

In India, the Gulabi Gang are an all-women vigilante force for women's rights, wearing pink saris and wielding bamboo sticks. Their founder was Sampat Pal Devi.

The daughter of a shepherd, Devi taught herself to read and write, and was married by the age of 12. At the age of 16, a nearby neighbour was regularly abusing his wife, and Devi decided to take action. She pleaded with the man to stop but he refused. The next day, Devi returned with a small group of women, all carrying sticks, and beat him as he had beaten his wife.

Other women in Devi's village and other villages joined the effort, and the movement grew, gaining tens of thousands of members spread over several districts in Uttar Pradesh, and later much of India. They became known as the 'Gulabi Gang', or 'Pink Gang', after the trademark pink saris they wear.

"Nobody comes to our help in these parts. The officials and the police are corrupt and anti-poor. So sometimes we have to take the law in our hands. At other times, we prefer to shame the wrongdoers," said Devi to the BBC in 2007.

The women arm themselves with lathi (a traditional Indian bamboo stick), which they use for self-defence whenever they come up against violent resistance.

They have carried out raids, including on police stations where the police have failed to act to protect women and girls, and beaten up several men and public officials.

In 2007, a woman of the 'lower' dalit caste was raped and the incident went unreported. Villagers and members of the lower caste protested, and many of them were put into prison for doing so. The Gulabi Gang took action, stormed into the police station and attempted to free the villagers who had been locked up for protesting. When a policeman refused to take action against the rapist, they resorted to violence and physically attacked him.

In 2008, the Gulabi Gang forced officials in an electricity office in Banda district to switch back on the power they had cut in order to extract bribes. They have also prevented child marriages and protested against dowry and female illiteracy.

A string of criminal charges and two stints in prison did not deter Devi from her aim of social justice and eliminating domestic violence. A chapter of the Gulabi Gang was even started in France.

Speaking to *The Guardian* newspaper in 2011, Devi said, "Village society in India is loaded against women. It refuses to educate them, marries them off too early, barters them for money. Village women need to study and become independent to sort it out themselves."

Sampat Pal Devi became well known across India, featuring on Indian reality TV show Bigg Boss – a move which was controversial with some of her followers. In March 2014, Sampat Pal Devi was expelled from the Gulabi Gang amidst allegations of being authoritarian and sacrificing interests of the movement for her personal political ambitions.

National convener of the Gulabi Gang, Jai Prakash Shivharey expressed his frustration with Devi: "Of late, she has become publicity crazy and has political ambitions of her own. The Gulabi Gang was formed to combat domestic violence, crime against women, corruption and inequality but Sampat Pal began using the organization to attain political power for herself. She contested the 2012 assembly elections without informing us and then went to the 'Bigg Boss' show on her own."

Al Jazeera reported in 2014 that the Gulabi Gang had an estimated 400,000 members, whereas the *Hindustan Times* put the figure at 270,000.

The Gulabi Gang is the subject of the 2010 movie *Pink Saris* and the 2012 documentary *Gulabi Gang*.

reddit referrer: fallenseraphim

Stetson Kennedy

Cleverly infiltrated and exposed the KKK

The American author and human rights activist Stetson Kennedy is possibly better-known than many people listed in this book, especially to US readers. But enough people are unaware of his role in the downfall of the Ku Klux Klan (KKK) that we just had to tell his story.

Kennedy was a life-long human rights activist – director of the Anti-Defamation League and Anti-Nazi League of New York during the 1940s. He also gave testimony in Geneva before the United Nations Commission on Forced Labour. But perhaps the most remarkable aspect of his life was his innovative and effective crusade to bring down the KKK.

"All my friends were in service and they were being shot at in a big way," said Kennedy, speaking of the time he was unable to join the WWII armed forces due to a back injury. "They were fighting racism whether they knew it or not. At least I could see if I could do something about the racist terrorists in our backyard."

Not one to shy away from danger, and with a conviction to promote human rights for all, Kennedy made it his goal to 'unmask' the KKK. On the basis that his then deceased uncle had been a member, he joined a local chapter, and got to work.

In the Grand Dragon's waste basket he found
financial documents and handed these over to
authorities. The KKK were forced to pay $685,000 in
tax. Kennedy leaked information about gatherings and
campaigns, causing headaches for Klan leaders, who
couldn't figure out how the information was being
discovered.

In the late 1940s, whilst working on the Superman
radio show, Kennedy saw an opportunity to raise his
game. Using his inside knowledge of the KKK's secret
codes, and rituals, Kennedy made the KKK Superman's
enemy. Dropping genuine facts into the show, the KKK's
arcane codes, rituals and racism were made a mockery
of, with Superman naturally triumphing over evil. The
radio shows are attributed as being instrumental in the
decline of the Klan in the US.

Kennedy wrote several books, including in the
1950s one called 'I Rode with the Ku Klux Klan' (later
renamed to 'The Klan Unmasked'). It exposed the rituals,
handshakes, costumes and folklore of the KKK – further
ridiculing their secrets. The book wasn't published
in full in the US until 1990. As late as 2011 Stetson
was still holding yet more confidential information
about the KKK – leaked documents which he called a
"ticking time bomb". This was released on his website
(stetsonkennedy.com).

Kennedy was proud of his role but always held some anxiety about reprisals. His dog was killed, and he was subject to numerous threats. In the end he lived until the grand old age of 94.

reddit referrer: DrRichardCranium

MEDICAL

*"Isn't it a bit unnerving that doctors
call what they do 'practice'?"*

– George Carlin

Inés Ramírez Pérez

Performed a caesarean section on herself

In March 2000, in a remote village in rural Mexico, Inés
Ramírez Pérez was heavily pregnant when, 12 hours
into labour, she began to experience great pain in her
abdomen. Having lost her previous unborn child at a late
stage of pregnancy, Ramírez was terrified that she was
about to lose another.

"When I was seven months pregnant with Orlando,
one night the pain began. It was terrible. I couldn't bear
it," Ramírez told reporters. "I started to panic. I knew I
had to do something or this baby would die too. I knew I
had to get it out somehow."

"I had seven children before Orlando," she said.
"There was no problem with the births. But the eighth
baby died. My waters broke and the midwife said I
needed a caesarean but I couldn't get to the hospital
in time. I felt the baby struggling but then it stopped
moving."

Immobilised by the pain, many miles from any
hospital, with only one phone in the town and her
husband out drinking in a cantina – she made an
incredible decision. She would deliver the baby herself,
by cutting open her own body.

With the pain growing worse, she sent her eight

year old son to buy a new kitchen knife from a local shop. "We had a knife but it wasn't that sharp," *The Independent* quoted her as saying.

In place of anaesthetic, she downed two cups of mezcal, a potent alcoholic Mexican drink, and began to cut at her abdomen. First slicing the skin, then fat and muscle, she had to move her internal organs to reach her uterus. "Blood came out of me like a fountain" she said. Finally she pulled out the baby, and to her relief heard her new son's first cries. She cut the umbilical cord, and tried to put her organs back where she had found them. "It was all a mess," she later said.

A local man helped stitch Ramírez back together using a regular sewing needle and thread, and then bundled her into a car. A 'local' clinic – one hour's drive away – immediately told her to go to San Pedro, location of the nearest hospital. This meant another two-hour drive but, in extreme agony, she finally made it.

Dr Onorio Galvan, head of the obstetrics department in the state hospital in San Pedro, was amazed at what he saw: "I couldn't believe it, there was no sepsis in the wound, no internal bleeding. She was back on her feet in a couple of days."

Thankfully, both mother and baby survived the ordeal, and were discharged ten days later.

On the 12-hour bus journey home, Ramírez grew

tired of the winding, bumpy journey, so left the bus and walked one-and-a-half hours along mountain footpaths to her village. "It was a short-cut," she explained.

Although there are historical accounts of other self-inflicted caesarians, it is thought that Ramírez is the first to have done this and survived. Her case was detailed in the March 2004 issue of the *International Journal of Gynecology & Obstetrics*.

When asked, she said she didn't advise other women to follow her example.

reddit referrer: sticksnstonesluv

George

Gunshot to the head cures mental illness

A young man's suicide attempt caused a brain injury which seemed to cure his mental illness whilst not causing any other damage.

Nineteen year old George suffered from Obsessive Compulsive Disorder and Clinical Depression, which made his life extremely difficult. His intense phobia of germs had caused obsessions which led him to spend hours each day showering and washing his hands. These symptoms resulted in him being forced to drop out of school and resign from his job. Psychiatrist Dr Leslie Solyom had been treating him for over a year with no lasting improvements.

The suicide attempt was the result of a conversation with George and his mother, where George told her that the extent of his depression was so great, he would rather die than be alive. His mother replied that if his life was so wretched, he should just go and shoot himself. George did just that, shooting a .22 rifle he had placed in his mouth in the basement of their house.

However, this did not have the desired effect of ending his life. Due to the angle that the gun was shot at, the bullet from the rifle ended up lodged in the front left lobe of George's brain. Surgeons operated to remove the bullet, but some fragments remained there, as it would have damaged the brain further to try and remove them, due to their positioning. Three weeks later, George was transferred to a psychiatric hospital, and by then almost all of his compulsions had gone, and his mood had improved considerably.

Following the incident, George returned to school, where he was a straight A student who went on to study at college. His IQ remained the same, but there was clearly a difference in his mental state, as he did not struggle with the mental illnesses which had had such a grip over his life before. This is not the first recorded case of brain injuries affecting mental state, but it is probably one of the most significant life-changing results of brain injury.

reddit referrer: tmos1985

Ali Maow Maalin

Hero of polio eradication

Polio is a highly contagious viral infection that can lead to paralysis and death. There is no cure. Until relatively recently polio used to be a big killer, but today polio has been eradicated in most countries, and many hope it will soon follow smallpox in being wiped out completely in the coming years.

Ali Maow Maalin was instrumental in Somalia's efforts to eradicate the disease.

In 1977, Maalin had the dubious honour of being the last person to contract a naturally occurring form of the smallpox virus. He was struck with the virus whilst working as a cook at Merka hospital. Fearing the needle would be painful, Maalin had avoided vaccination pretending he'd already received the shot. Fortunately, the smallpox strain he contracted was a weaker one, and he made a full recovery.

After recovering, Maalin vowed not to let others make the same potentially deadly mistake, and he joined the effort to rid his country of another virus, polio.

Maalin became heavily involved in the polio eradication efforts in his country, joining thousands of other volunteers. As a local coordinator for the World Health Organization (WHO), Maalin travelled throughout Somalia encouraging parents in communities to immunise their children against polio. His personal story was an especially powerful narrative in persuading fellow Somalis to vaccinate their children.

In a 2006 Boston Globe article Maalin explained his effectiveness by saying, "Now when I meet parents who refuse to give their children the polio vaccine, I tell them my story. I tell them how important these vaccines are. I tell them not to do something foolish like me."

Speaking to the BBC, Maalin said: "Somalia was the last country with smallpox. I wanted to help ensure that we would not be the last place with polio too."

reddit referrer: lfairy

Ashik Gavai

The boy who had 232 teeth removed

In 2014, Indian teenager Ashik Gavai was taken from his rural village to doctors in Mumbai after suffering for 18 months from pain and swelling in his mouth. Local doctors had been unable to diagnose the problem.

Dr Sunanda Dhiware, head of Mumbai's JJ Hospital's dental department, told the BBC, "Ashik's malaise was diagnosed as a complex composite odontoma where a single gum forms lots of teeth. It's a sort of benign tumour."

"Once we opened it, little pearl-like teeth started coming out, one-by-one. Initially, we were collecting them, they were really like small white pearls. But then we started to get tired. We counted 232 teeth," she added.

"According to medical literature available on the condition, it is known to affect the upper jaw and a maximum of 37 teeth have been extracted from the tumour in the past. But in Ashik's case, the tumour was found deep in the lower jaw and it had hundreds of teeth."

Gavai had to endure seven hours of medics pulling teeth from his mouth, and despite the doctors' fears, his jaw remained intact. The cost of the surgery was covered by the state government's health insurance scheme.

At an incredible 232 teeth removed, this is thought to be a world record.

Following the procedure, Ashik Gavai was left with a 'normal' 28 teeth.

reddit referrer: themetz

Charles Osborne

Hiccupped continuously for 68 years

Charles Osborne's hiccups began in 1922, after a 350-pound hog collapsed on top of him while he was preparing to slaughter it. His hiccuping persisted for 68 years, about one hic every 10 seconds.

It is speculated that either an abdomen muscle was pulled or a blood vessel in the brain burst and destroyed the part of the brain stem that inhibits hiccups. Operations were attempted to stop the hiccups, without success. Hormone therapy stopped the hiccups for 36 hours, but was stopped due to other health complications.

Osborne's condition led him to be a guest on the New York radio show *Ripley's Believe It or Not!* in 1936 and *The Tonight Show Starring Johnny Carson* in 1983. He was also featured as a question in the board game *Trivial Pursuit.*

The hiccups stopped when Osborne was 97. He died a year later.

Osborne is in *Guinness World Records* as the man with the Longest Attack of Hiccups (68 years, between 1922–1990).

reddit referrer: last0nethere

Dr Bon Verweij

The surgeon who gave a woman a 3D-printed skull

Dr Bon Verweij led a team which operated on an (unnamed) patient suffering from chronic bone disorder, a condition which meant that her skull had grown to a thickness of five centimetres as opposed to the normal 2.5 centimetres. This was causing significant health problems because the skull was pressing down on her brain tissue, causing symptoms such as degradation of vision and cognitive functions. If left untreated, the condition would very likely have led to certain brain damage, and potentially caused death.

Anatomics, an Australian firm, were responsible for creating this transparent plastic cranium, which was custom built out of durable plastic to the exact specifications necessary. The team at the University Medical Centre Utrecht removed the top hemisphere of the patient's skull, and replaced it with the version made by 3D printing. Titanium clasps and screws attached this new plastic cranium, and the hemisphere of the skull was replaced on top of the implant. It is not yet known whether a replacement skull will be needed at a later stage in the patient's life.

Whilst 3D printing has begun to be used in more cases, such as replacing tracheas, this is thought to be the largest 3D implant which has ever occurred. It is also the first skull to have ever been transplanted.

The 23 hour long operation was extremely successful, and the patient has recovered sufficiently enough to be able to go back to work. Those involved hope that this procedure will be able to be used more in future with other bone problems, whether they are the result of a condition or an accident.

Commenting on the procedure, Verweij says that it "has major advantages, not only cosmetically, but also because patients often have better brain function compared with the old method".

reddit referrer: hinesh

Hu Songwen

Created his own dialysis machine

Hu Songwen was diagnosed with kidney failure in 1993, when he was a student, which meant his kidneys could not remove toxic waste products from his blood unaided. One in ten Chinese people are unable to afford dialysis for life-threatening kidney problems, and Hu was soon to become one of this number. For six years his family managed to fund the $80 hospital dialysis that he required at least every six days. However, when the money ran out, Hu did not give in. Instead, he proceeded to make his own dialysis machine, which he could use from home at a much cheaper price.

Undeterred by the knowledge that he had two friends who had died from using dialysis machines they had created themselves, Hu went about creating his own dialysis machine using kitchen utensils and disused medical equipment. It works in the same way as any other dialysis machine, as the blood is removed from the body via tubes, and the excess potassium and sodium are removed from the blood due to being diffused through a membrane and dialysis fluid, meaning the blood can then be returned to the body. Hu creates the dialysis fluid himself, using potassium chloride, sodium chloride, sodium hydrogen carbonate and purified water. This home treatment costs only twelve per cent of the cost of each hospital treatment he used to pay for.

Since a report of this self-treatment was published, Hu has been offered government medical funding for his dialysis. However, the nearest hospital is overcrowded and difficult to reach, so despite the doctors' warnings of the dangers of infection from using water that has not been sterilised, Hu continues to use his machine for dialysis. He explains: "As long as you have a high school degree, understand the principle of dialysis, follow the operational instructions and keep a close watch during the process, nothing should go wrong."

Hu has survived off this homemade dialysis machine for thirteen years now, and still continues to have no problems from it.

reddit referrer: slapyomamah

Ignaz Semmelweiss

Saved millions of lives through hand washing

Ignaz Semmelweiss was a Hungarian doctor who was the first to realise the importance of clean hands in preventing infection.

Whilst working in the maternity section of The Vienna General Hospital in the 1840s, Semmelweiss became aware of the number of deaths that were due to puerperal fever after childbirth, more commonly known as childbed fever. The hospital had two maternity wards, with the First Clinic having a mortality rate which could reach 30%, while the Second Clinic had a much lower mortality rate of around 4%. This was a cause of concern for Semmelweiss, as he realised women who were aware of this would rather have their babies on the street outside than be admitted to the First Clinic. It was commonly thought that the problems of the First Clinic were due to overcrowding, or 'poisonous gas' in the air, which was the widely accepted theory of disease at the time. Both clinics were run in the exact same way, with the only difference being that the First Clinic was where medical students and doctors who worked in all areas treated women, but only midwives were allowed to be present in the Second Clinic.

Semmelweiss realised that the midwives were only

working with the pregnant women, whereas the medical students and doctors could be moving straight from performing post-mortems on dead bodies to helping deliver babies. In 1847, one of Semmelweiss's colleagues died as a result of septicaemia after accidentally being cut with a scalpel whilst performing a post-mortem. Semmelweiss believed that the scalpel had transferred something from the dead body to his colleague, which caused the death. As a result, he instructed all the medical students and doctors working in the First Clinic to wash their hands with a solution of chlorinated lime before treating any patient. Mortality rates in the First Clinic immediately dropped from 10% to 2%. However, his ideas were ridiculed, and it was only after his death that scientists realised the importance of his discovery, and hand-washing became implemented in hospitals.

reddit referrer: grendel001

James Harrison

He single-handedly saved the lives of over two million unborn babies

James had to undergo hospital procedures at the age of 13, and remained in hospital for several months after, resulting in him requiring 13 litres of blood. He was aware that the blood he had received had saved his life, and therefore was determined to start giving blood himself when he reached the age of 18.

His first donation was in 1954, and soon after he was discovered to be of the rare blood group, $Rh_o(D)$. This means his blood plasma – the fluid in which our red and white blood cells are carried – carries a rare antibody which is given to women during and after pregnancy, in order to prevent Rhesus disease in newborns. When James began donating, Rhesus disease, a severe form of anaemia, was causing a serious problem in Australia, with thousands of newborns dying, and many being brain damaged as a result of it.

After the large proportion of these antibodies was discovered in his blood, James' body was insured for one million Australian dollars, showing how vital the antibody was proving to be for women and newborns.

James' blood has also led to the development of a vaccination, which is given to all pregnant women who are Rh negative. One in ten women are given this vaccination, especially if they have blood which may not be compatible with that of their child's, as a parent with Rhesus positive blood cannot be compatible with a child of Rhesus negative blood, and vice versa.

James' blood has been given to thousands of women, including his own daughter, and has allowed many women to have babies who have survived where this would not have been possible before.

Now in his seventies, James still donates regularly every few weeks. This frequency is possible as he only needs to donate blood plasma, not the oxygen-carrying red blood cells. Even being on holiday does not stop him, as he will simply donate at the nearest available place.

At the time of writing, the 74 year old has given blood over one thousand times.

"I've never thought about stopping. Never," he said. Even after the passing of his wife of 56 years, Harrison remains dedicated to donating his blood plasma.

"It was sad but life marches on and we have to continue doing what we do. She's up there looking down, so I carry on."

reddit referrer: TryHardDieHard

Man with less than half a brain

...and he's a civil servant

In 2007, a 44-year-old Frenchman (whose name has not been released) went to his local hospital complaining of weakness in his leg. Examining his medical records, doctors discovered that the man had suffered from a build-up of fluid in his skull as a young child, and to drain the fluid a shunt had been fitted. The shunt was removed when he was 14.

"He was a married father of two children, and worked as a civil servant," Dr Lionel Feuillet and colleagues at the Université de la Méditerranée in Marseille wrote, in a letter to *The Lancet* medical journal.

Scans were performed on the man's brain. What they revealed astonished the medical team. The majority of the area where the brain should have been, was taken up by a huge fluid-filled chamber.

"It is hard for me to say exactly the percentage of reduction of the brain, since we did not use software to measure its volume. But visually, it is more than a 50% to 75% reduction," said Feuillet, when speaking to *New Scientist*.

Despite such a dramatic reduction in brain volume, the man scored 84 on a verbal IQ test and 70 on a performance IQ test. This is lower than the average of 100, but still within the 'normal' range, and far more than might be expected.

Commenting on the remarkable scan images, Siri Graff Leknes, brain researcher at the University of Oslo, said: "If a photo like that had landed in my hands without my knowing anything about the person, I'd have guessed the individual was nearly dead."

"If something happens very slowly over quite some time, maybe over decades, the different parts of the brain take up functions that would normally be done by the part that is pushed to the side," commented Dr Max Muenke, a paediatric brain defect specialist at the National Human Genome Research Institute.

News agency Reuters couldn't resist covering the story with a headline punning the man's: *'Tiny brain no obstacle to French civil servant'*.

reddit referrer: lilygal

Timothy Brown

The first person to be cured of HIV

In 1995, while at school in Berlin, Timothy Brown was diagnosed with HIV. For the next 11 years, doctors kept his HIV under control using anti-retroviral therapy.

In 2006, however, Brown developed leukaemia – with no connection to HIV. His first round of treatment seemed to bring positive results, but it also made him more susceptible to infections. As a consequence, Brown developed pneumonia, followed later by sepsis. His doctors were forced to try a different approach.

To treat the leukaemia, Brown's oncologist, Dr Gero Hütter, who was then with the Free University of Berlin, chose a stem cell transplant using a healthy donor (Brown is sometimes referred to as 'The Berlin Patient'). But this was not a typical donor – the individual was chosen as they had a mutation that makes cells immune to HIV, and Dr Hütter reasoned that the immunity may be transferred to Brown.

Intense chemotherapy was used to kill Brown's own immune system, and whole-body irradiation prepared him for a bone marrow transplant – the origin of his leukaemia. The stem cells from the donor were then transplanted to initiate growth of new bone marrow. Results showed that the transplant not only treated

Brown's leukaemia but had also eliminated the HIV from his system.

Brown claims to have not needed anti-retrovirals since the procedure, but one drawback of his treatment was neurological damage. "There was a period after my transplant when I couldn't even walk," he said.

Timothy Brown is believed to be the only known patient who was once infected with the HIV virus and is now clear. He has volunteered for numerous studies to aid HIV research.

reddit referrer: SledDave

Walter Williams

Waking the dead

Seventy-eight year old Walter Williams from Mississippi was discovered dead by members of his family and his hospice nurse one evening in February 2014. Naturally distraught, they telephoned coroner Dexter Howard, who immediately left for Walter's home, and on finding no pulse in his body, proclaimed him dead at 9pm that evening.

After completing the necessary paperwork, Howard transported Walter's body to Porter and Sons Funeral Home in a body bag. It was when the body bag had been placed in the embalming room that Howard noticed it beginning to move.

Walter's legs visibly began to kick, and he also appeared to be starting to breathe. An ambulance was called, and paramedics discovered Walter to have a heartbeat where none had been found before. He was transported to the nearby Holmes County Hospital, and attached to monitors, where he was weak, but alive. Walter was released to go home a few days later.

Doctors at the hospital speculated that Walter's vital signs may have appeared unresponsive as a result of the combination of medication that he was taking at the time. The coroner, Howard believes the only explanation can be that the defibrillator, which was attached to Walter's body under his skin, had caused Walter's heart to start again.

Whilst there have been recorded cases of people believed to be dead coming back to life, this has never knowingly been the result of a defibrillator. Howard reasons that "It could've kicked in, started his heart back... the bottom line is it's a miracle."

Indeed, Walter's family regarded it as a miracle, as nephew Hester who was the one to inform the coroner on discovering his uncle explained: "I don't know how long he's going to be here, but I know he's back right now. That's all that matters."

You might think this was an isolated incident, but it wasn't. In January 2014 a 24-year-old Kenyan, Paul Mutora, was pronounced dead after swallowing insecticide. Sent to the morgue, he woke 15 hours later, causing staff to "take to their heels, screaming". Later the same year, Janina Kolkiewicz, a 91-year-old Polish woman, woke up in a morgue after being declared dead. She had been refrigerated for 11 hours.

So, although it is rare, it does happen. In part this is because death can be surprisingly difficult to diagnose; there are many conditions which emulate death, without an individual actually dying. In the case of Walter Williams, coroner Howard had no medical degree, leading some to argue that this contributed to the misdiagnosis. In fact, coroners in many US states are not required to have a medical degree. The same is true for UK coroners, but they are not given powers to pronounce people dead.

Let's not think too long about the individuals we never get to learn about who wake up in the morgue and don't get discovered...

reddit referrer: Webguy55

SPORT

"You have to give 100 percent in the first half of the game. If that isn't enough, in the second half, you have to give what's left."

–Yogi Berra

Frank Hayes and Ralph Neves

A dead cert winner and a second chance

Jockey Frank Hayes was a surprise 20-1 winner at Belmont Park, USA, in 1923. Hayes wasn't even a jockey – he was really a horse trainer and stableman, but had persuaded the owner of a horse to let him ride.

The only problem was that half-way round the course he had died of a heart attack. Hayes' body remained in the saddle throughout the race, so that when *Sweet Kiss* eventually crossed the finish line, Hayes was still sat in the saddle.

It was only after race officials came to congratulate the winner did anyone realise that Hayes had died.

Three days later, Hayes was buried wearing his jockey outfit.

After this, no one wanted to ride the horse, and a nickname quickly emerged: 'Sweet Kiss of Death'. Hayes became the first and, as far as we know, only jockey known to have won a race after death.

However, thirteen years later another jockey came pretty close …

On 8th May 1936, 19-year-old Ralph Neves was competing in a race at Bay Meadows Racetrack in San Mateo, California, when he fell and was crushed by his horse. The track physician declared Neves dead, and his body was taken to a nearby hospital. As a last effort to revive him before being sent to the mortuary, Neves was injected with adrenaline. Miraculously, he lept up and jumped in a taxi straight back to the race track where he astounded the crowd and officials by demanding to be allowed to finish his races.

Not surprisingly, he wasn't allowed to race again that day, but the next day he was back on his horse. Neves continued to ride until his retirement in 1964. At the time of his second and final death in 1995, aged 78, Neves had won 3,772 races and had been honoured in both the United States Racing Hall of Fame and the Washington Racing Hall of Fame.

reddit referrer: cmd194

Alysia Montaño

Ran the 800m at the US Track and Field Championships while 34 weeks pregnant

On 26th June 2014, Alysia Montaño completed a task many mothers might believe to be impossible. Montaño competed in the 800m at the US Track and Field Championships despite being heavily pregnant – only six weeks away from the due date of her first child. She finished the race in last place with a time of two minutes, 32.13 seconds to the cheers and applause of the crowds who gave her a standing ovation in acknowledgement of her achievement.

Montaño, who had won the 800m national title for the previous four years, said that she had trained throughout her pregnancy with the encouragement of doctors: "I've been running throughout my pregnancy and I felt really, really good during the whole process."

Initially Montaño expressed fears of becoming the first athlete to be lapped in the 800m, but although she lagged at least 120 metres behind her competitors for the majority of the race, she never came close to being lapped and crossed the line as an inspiration to professional women athletes all round the world.

Montaño gave birth to a daughter in August 2014.

reddit referrer: 5kl

Bryan Heitkotter

From gamer to racer

Most people who have raced cars in video games have, at some point or other, imagined themselves at the wheels of a true race car. Bryan Heitkotter turned these dreams into reality – from Gran Turismo gamer to a real-life member of Nissan's racing team.

This amazing transformation came about thanks to a 2011 competition launched in the US, which was designed to give the best video game racer a shot at becoming a professional race car driver.

Over 53,000 people applied to take part in the GT Academy – online time trials in Gran Turismo 5, organised by PlayStation, Gran Turismo, and Nissan. Thirty-two of the best players in the US made it to the National Finals event in Orlando in March. A shortlist of 16 finalists were taken to the UK's Silverstone race track, where they faced a week of training and racing.

Racing industry veterans judged the racers, and after intense competition, Bryan Heitkotter from California was crowned the first US winner of GT Academy.

"The week at Silverstone was full-throttle intense," Heitkotter explained to gamer website *Polygon*. "We contestants were given so much advice and instruction that it wasn't easy to take it all in and retain everything during the week. As always in a learning experience, some things stick with you better than others."

"Racing video games were my fix growing up," remembers Heitkotter. "I lived my racing career many times over, vicariously through the screen. It was the closest I thought I would ever get at times, and yet sometimes I felt that somehow, some way, I would get into racing in real life. But I didn't know how."

Heitkotter returned to England for intensive training on Nissan's six-month 'Driver Development Program'. In 2012 he raced professionally at the Indianapolis Motor Speedway, setting a qualifying record and earning pole position. The same year Heitkotter and his team finished third in the *24 Hours of Dubai* race. In his team were other GT Academy winners, European 2010 champion Jann Mardenborough, 2010 GT Academy winner Jordan Tresson, and 2008 GT Academy winner Lucas Ordoñez.

"Although I've realised my dream of becoming a racing driver, it doesn't end there. My long term goal is to have a lasting career in the sport, and that doesn't come easy," he concluded.

reddit referrer: imbignate

Cliff Young

The 61 year old farmer who ran 544 mile ultra-marathon

In 1983, when Cliff Young turned up to compete in the long-distance race from Sydney to Melbourne, the other competitors looked on with amusement. They were all world-class athletes, with corporate backing and mostly under 30 years of age. Cliff Young, however, was a 61 year old farmer whose training consisted of rounding up sheep. He turned up in his overalls and work boots.

The Australian endurance race usually took at least seven days, over flats and hills, and competitors were allowed to eat and sleep when they wanted – most athletes aimed to run 18 hours a day and sleep the remaining six. The first person to reach the finish picked up the $10,000 prize.

When the race started, Cliff Young was quickly left behind by the other competitors. To make matters worse, he didn't appear to be running – his technique was more of a shuffle. Each night, though, as the other athletes slept, Young carried on shuffling, and by the final night, he had overtaken all the runners. He crossed the finish line first, with a time of five days, 15 hours and four minutes – a full 10 hours ahead of the nearest competitor, and breaking the previous race record by more than two days.

Although no one else had believed he was capable, right from the start Cliff Young was confident he could finish the race. He said: "I grew up on a farm where we couldn't afford horses or tractors and the whole time I was growing up, whenever the storms would roll in, I'd have to go out and round up the sheep. We had 2,000 sheep on 2,000 acres. Sometimes I would have to run those sheep for two or three days. It took a long time, but I'd always catch them."

And his running technique? Well, the 'Young shuffle' has now been adopted by ultra-marathon runners because it is considered more energy efficient.

reddit referrer: ndyrg2

Derek Derenalagi

Declared dead, then competed in the Paralympics

In July 2007, Fiji-born Derek Derenalagi was serving with the British army in Helmand Province, Afghanistan. It was his second tour.

He was in his Land Rover when the vehicle's right tyre rolled over an improvised explosive device – a large drum buried beneath the ground, loaded with explosives, ball bearings, nails and a pressure sensor. The explosion ripped through the vehicle, badly injuring Derenalagi. Doctors fought to save his life, but eventually declared him dead.

Medical staff were about to put him into a body bag when, amazingly, one doctor detected a weak pulse.

Derenalagi was operated on, including amputating both legs below the knee, and he was then flown to the UK. In a coma for the next two weeks, he finally woke to find his wife, Ana, at his bedside. Derenalagi asked if he could go to the bathroom, and Ana had to explain that he couldn't, because he had lost his legs. Derek was in disbelief: "I couldn't believe it because I could feel that I still had my boots on and my feet were very warm."

With great resolve, and the help of the British army's 'Battle Back' rehabilitation programme, Derenalagi spent the following years training to be a proud Paralympian, playing sitting volleyball as well as discus, javelin and shot put.

Five years after being declared dead, Derenalagi competed for Great Britain in the 2012 Paralympics in London. He received a hero's welcome as he entered the stadium.

Emma Parry, founder of the UK's 'Help for Heroes' charity spoke to *The Daily Telegraph* in 2012 about Derenalagi. "It was devastating for both of us to see somebody so injured when we visited him in hospital," Emma recalled. "But to see him five years later, having battled everything to get through to the Paralympics, is absolutely extraordinary."

At the 2012 IPC Athletics European Championships, Derenalagi won the gold medal in the F57/58 discus. In the final round of the competition, his winning throw of 41.41 metres (135.9 ft) was enough to beat Russian F58 world champion and world record holder Alexey Ashapatov.

Derenalagi still recounts the words he spoke moments after his horrific injury: "I said, 'Lord Jesus Christ, if you are willing to use my life to motivate and encourage others, then please give me life again'."

reddit user: user's account no longer active

Shavarsh Karapetyan

World-record swimmer and heroic lifesaver

Eleven-times world record-breaker, 17 times world champion finswimmer and 13 times European champion – Armenian Shavarsh Karapetyan's story is an incredible tale of sporting achievement and heroism.

When he was 15, he narrowly escaped drowning after getting into a fight with a group of youths who beat him, tied a heavy stone to his neck, threw him into a lake and left him. Karapetyan managed to untie his hands, remove the weight from his neck and swam to the surface. In an interview he later said, "If the stone was slightly heavier, I would not have been able to get out of the water."

Following this incident, Karapetyan decided to take swimming lessons. A natural talent, he soon started to compete professionally. Without a coach, he became a champion of Armenia at the age of 17. He then switched to finswimming and within 12 months he became the champion of the Soviet Union, followed two months later by breaking the world record as the European champion.

During a competition in Kiev, his oxygen tanks were tampered with, the culprit thought to be a fellow competitor. Running out of oxygen meant Karapetyan had to swim 75 metres whilst holding his breath. He managed to win the race, but lost consciousness and was hospitalised.

His next scrape with death occurred not in the pool, but on the way to it. In 1974 Karapetyan was on his morning bus commute through mountain roads when the driver collapsed and the bus was about to plummet. With just inches to spare, Karapetyan jumped into the driver's seat and averted danger. Thirty lives were saved.

In 1976, Karapetyan was coming towards the end of a 12-mile run with his brother, alongside the Yerevan Lake, when they heard a loud crash. A trolleybus filled with 92 passengers had fallen from a dam and was sinking more than 30ft to the bottom of the reservoir. Karapetyan immediately dived in, breaking the rear window with his legs. In near-darkness, he extracted passengers, one-by-one. Working frantically, Karapetyan managed to save 20 people.

The combined effect of cold water and the multiple lacerations he received from the broken glass – plus sepsis from the raw sewage in the lake water – left him unconscious for 45 days. This marked the end of his sports career.

He eventually became a nationwide hero. He was awarded the Order of the Badge of Honour by the USSR, and another medal 'For Saving Drowning People in the

Water'. In 1978 an asteroid was named after him: *3027 Shavarsh.*

In 1985, yet another life-threatening incident saw him rescuing a number of people from a burning building. Which again put him in hospital.

Karapetyan took part in the 2014 Winter Olympics torch relay, from Moscow towards Krasnogorsk. The next day, he carried the torch for a second time. "I was carrying the torch for Russia and for Armenia," he said in an interview.

Karapetyan was awarded a UNESCO 'Fair Play' award for his heroism. He now lives in Moscow, where he founded a running shoe company.

reddit referrer: SnugNinja

Steven Bradbury

The most unexpected gold medal in history?

At the 2002 Salt Lake Winter Olympics, one gold medal winner was luckier than most. Or was it luck? Competing in the short track speed skating event, Bradbury won his heat convincingly; however, in the quarter-finals he was up against two of the world's best – USA's Apolo Anton Ohno, and Marc Gagnon of Canada, the defending World Champion. Only the fastest two from each race would proceed to the semi-finals. Bradbury finished third but Gagnon was disqualified for obstructing another racer. So Bradbury was through to the semis.

Working with Ann Zhang, his coach, Bradbury opted for a strategy of 'sitting back', observing that the faster racers were taking big risks. He hoped to capitalise on this by avoiding being caught in a pile-up. During the semi-final Bradbury was well off the pace of the medal favourites, but when three skaters collided, he was able to take second place. The strategy had worked again.

Coming into the five-man final, Australia's Steven Bradbury was the rank outsider, and as the race progressed he fell towards the rear of the pack.

As a tense battle emerged ahead of him, Bradbury fought to maintain position. As his competitors jostled for first position on the final bend, Lia Jiajun of China went to overtake Ohno. The manoeuvre proved disastrous. Within a split second the first four skaters tumbled into each other and spun on the ice. Not quite believing his luck, a shocked Bradbury raised his arms and sailed across the line as the gold medalist.

"I was the oldest bloke in the field and I knew that, skating four races back to back, I wasn't going to have any petrol left in the tank," said Bradbury after the semi-final. "So there was no point in getting there and mixing it up because I was going to be in last place anyway. So (I figured) I might as well stay out of the way and be in last place and hope that some people get tangled up."

Interviewed after winning gold, Bradbury said, "Obviously I wasn't the fastest skater. I don't think I'll take the medal as the minute-and-a-half of the race I actually won. I'll take it as the last decade of the hard slog I put in."

Bradbury retired from competitive speed skating after the 2002 Olympics, becoming a commentator and later starting a new career as a race car driver in Australia.

reddit referrer: earthtoannie

WAR

"War does not determine who is right – only who is left."

– Bertrand Russell

Juan Pujol Garcia

The greatest double-agent on Earth

Influenced by his experiences during his country's civil war, Spaniard Juan Pujol Garcia was an anti-fascist with great aspirations to be a spy, but with no experience or training in espionage. In 1941, undeterred by his lack of credentials, Pujol went to the British embassy in Madrid, and offered his services as a spy. Described by a British expert on military history as a "balding, boring and unsmiling little man", he was turned down.

Unwilling to give up his dreams of becoming a spy, Pujol swiftly changed tactics and offered his services to the Germans instead, claiming that he was a Nazi sympathizer working for the Spanish government who made frequent trips to London. The lie was outrageous: not only did he not speak a work of English, but far from working in the government, Pujol's previous job had involved chicken farming and managing a one star hotel in Madrid. Still, he forged a diplomatic passport to support his story and the Germans were fooled. They gave him an intense course in espionage and set him to work recruiting English agents who could send dispatches back to Germany.

Since both his passport and employment were fake, Pujol carried out orders to spy in England from Lisbon in Portugal. There, he created fictional agents using a guidebook of England to make his characters' positions and movements sound convincing. Pujol also read many books about the British Military, and English magazines in order to make the entirely made-up information he passed on to the Nazis sound believable.

So successful was he in convincing the Germans that he was a real spy that they took his reports very seriously. When they made a dramatic response to a completely imaginary Pujol lead, that British troops were active in Malta, British intelligence finally paid the 'balding, boring' Pujol some attention. Having started to notice Pujol's reports and actions from little snippets picked up in radio communications, it was his Malta stunt that swayed the Brits. They found him, moved him to London, and made him an agent.

Now working alongside the British, Pujol could send real reports of unimportant troop movements back to Germany and his credibility was asserted by crucial bits of information sent, just too late to be of any use to the Nazis. These deliberately late reports included the warning that British Troops would invade North Africa in November 1942 to which the Nazis responded, "We are sorry they arrived too late but your last reports were magnificent."

Perhaps Pujol's greatest achievement as a double

agent was his success in deceiving Hitler that the Allies would land at Pas de Calais for the D-Day landings, rather than in Normandy. As part of the ruse, the Allies stationed American General George Patton in Dover and Pujol convinced Hitler, by extensive communications from his 'agents' and confusing reports, that huge swathes of troops were gathering at Dover and preparing to sail for Calais. Even as the first ships began to land on the Normandy beaches, Pujol's credibility as a loyal Nazi asset was such that his urgent reports that the attack was only to draw attentions away from the true attack which would take place at Calais, led Hitler to order for troops heading to Normandy to turn back.

Even two months after the D-Day attack at Normandy, German troops remained stationed at Calais, waiting for the 'true' attack that Pujol had convinced them would happen.

Pujol's success as a double agent resulted in remarkable honours from both England and Germany; receiving an MBE from King George VI and the Iron Cross from Hitler. After the war, Pujol's death was faked to protect him from Nazi sympathisers and he retired to Venezuela to live out the rest of his life running a small gift shop. He died in 1988, aged 76.

reddit referrer: potato1

Chiune Sugihara

Japanese diplomat who saved the lives of several thousand Jews during the Second World War

Working at the Japanese Consulate in Lithuania in 1939, Chiune Sugihara became inundated with requests for visas from Jewish refugees who had left Poland due to the threat posed to them by the Nazis. No travel was possible without a visa, but many countries were too afraid to issue them, and many of the refugees who applied for them lacked the necessary requirements to be granted one – immigrants had to have sufficient money and have gone through appropriate immigration procedures. Sugihara asked for instructions from the Japanese foreign ministry several times, and was told each time that anyone who asked for a visa would also need to show a visa to exit Japanese territory for another country.

Through 1940, the threat of the situation for Jews grew, and Sugihara took matters into his own hands. Ignoring government protocol, he granted visas off his own initiative, disobeying orders and giving Jews a ten-day travel permit through Japan. From there, they would be able to go on to China or elsewhere. From 31st July to 28th August, Sugihara and his wife issued thousands of visas, often staying up until late in the night in order to write more. A common day would see them issuing a month's worth of visas; such was the extent they went to in an attempt to save people.

The closure of the Japanese Consulate forced Sugihara and his family to move, yet even as they were waiting for the train to leave, he and his wife were still writing visas and handing them out of the window. It is thought that at least six thousand Jews were able to escape due to their work.

After returning to Japan, Sugiahara was forced to resign, which is thought to be a result of handing out the unauthorised visas. He never spoke of the visas, and little was known of them until a survivor made contact with him in 1968. He was then widely acclaimed, and granted the honour of The Righteous Among Nations.

There are thought to be 40,000 people alive today due to the visas that Sughihara and his wife issued. When asked about his reasoning for issuing the visas, Chiune Sugihara responded: "I myself thought this would be the right thing to do. There is nothing wrong in saving many people's lives."

Also see *Irena Sendler.*

reddit referrer: Squeenis

Edith Cavell

First World War nurse, whose execution caused international outrage

Before the war, Edith Cavell was a matron of a nursing hospital in Brussels, which was then taken over by the Red Cross following the outbreak of war. From November 1914, the Germans occupied Belgium, taking over the hospital where she worked. The Germans sent most English nurses home, but Edith was one of the few chosen to remain. As the clinic then became a Red Cross Hospital, it was of great importance that all patients were treated with the same level of care, irrespective of their nationality, because the Red Cross were expected to be neutral in their treatment and views.

However, in 1914, two stranded British soldiers appeared at the hospital, and Edith sheltered them until they could be transported to the Netherlands – neutral territory. This continued, with British and French soldiers being regularly hidden by Edith until there was a safe place to transport them to. In total, Edith helped 60 British soldiers, 15 French soldiers, and 100 Belgium men of military age to safety.

This was illegal behaviour from Edith, as it breached both German law and the Red Cross conduct which she was held under as a nurse in the hospital.

Edith's actions were betrayed, and on 3rd August
1915, she was arrested and held in prison for ten weeks.
Under pressure from deliberately leading questions at
her trial, and the false information from others involved,
she admitted to aiding the escape of French and British
soldiers.

German law meant the penalty for this was death,
and in times of war, the laws applied to foreigners as
well. There was nothing the British government could
do to help her. The night before her execution, Edith
is reported to have said, "Patriotism is not enough. I
must have no hatred or bitterness towards anyone."
Her execution was carried out by firing squad, on the
morning of 12th October 1915.

reddit referrer: NMW

Eric 'Winkle' Brown

Record-breaking British pilot whose unique skillset gave him a crucial role in the Second World War

Captain Eric Brown is probably the greatest test pilot in history, having flown more different aircraft types than anyone else. Along the way he broke records and, due in part to his fluent German, got to interrogate leading Nazis.

Eric Brown, a Scot, was hooked on flying early. Aged just eight, he was taken up in a biplane by his father, an ex-Royal Flying Corps WWI pilot.

In 1936, his father took him to see the Olympics in Berlin, where they met with members of the then newly-formed Luftwaffe. It was there that he met Ernst Udet, a German former World War I fighter ace, who offered to take Brown up for a flight. "He subjected me to some pretty hairy aerobatics," Brown told the BBC in 2013, "then frightened the life out of me by coming in to land upside down – only at the last minute did he turn the aircraft over. We literally fell onto the runway."

Impressed with Brown's ability to cope with the aerobatics, Udet gave Brown the German fighter pilot salute "Hals- und Beinbruch!" meaning "Break your neck and legs". Udet urged Brown to learn to fly, saying that he "had the temperament of a fighter pilot". He also suggested that Brown should learn to speak German.

Suitably impressed, Brown followed Udet's advice, deciding the next year to study German at Edinburgh University (a language skill that would later prove very useful), and joining the university's flight school – where his formal air training began.

In 1939, Brown was on an exchange course in Germany when war was declared with the UK. The SS arrested Brown, and escorted him to the Swiss border. Luckily, he was free to return home. Had the SS known of Brown's piloting skills, the outcome may have been different.

Back in the UK, he became a pilot in the Royal Navy Volunteer Reserve, and his first post was with *HMS Audacity*. Originally built as a German merchant ship, *Audacity* was subsequently captured by British forces and converted into an escort carrier – essentially a small aircraft carrier. While with *Audacity* Brown shot down two German Focke-Wulf 'Condor' maritime patrol aircraft.

In 1941 *Audacity* was torpedoed by a U-boat, and rapidly sank. Brown was in a group of 28 initial survivors who clung to each other in the cold waters. One by one through the night that followed, the men slipped into unconsciousness and drowned. By the morning, Brown was one of just two survivors. The experience haunts him to this day.

The following year, Brown was awarded the Distinguished Service Cross for his service on *Audacity*, "for bravery and skill in action against enemy aircraft and in the protection of a convoy against heavy and sustained enemy attacks".

By this time, Brown – nicknamed 'Winkle' due to his short stature – had built up considerable expertise in deck landings, a much sought-after skill. Because of this, he was posted at the Royal Aircraft Establishment (RAE) at Farnborough to work as a test pilot on the new breed of British naval aircraft – the Sea Hurricane and Seafire. By the end of 1943 he had clocked up around 1,500 deck landings on 22 different carriers. He used his expertise to help train the Royal Canadian Air Force in carrier landing techniques, and he flew with Fighter Command in the air defence of Great Britain.

In 1943 Brown returned to the RAE as chief test pilot. Whilst there he continued to push the boundaries of what was possible with flight technology. That year he made the first ever landing on a carrier by a twin-engined aircraft, and flew modified Spitfires in high speed dives close to the speed of sound. He was also involved in evaluating captured enemy planes which, repainted in British RAF insignia, must have made a confusing sight flying over the skies of southern England.

In his six years at Farnborough he hardly ever took a single day's leave. His house was destroyed by a V1 'doodlebug' bomb; Brown was not at home but his wife was concussed and their cleaner lost an eye.

In 1944 he was appointed Member of the Order of the British Empire (MBE) "for outstanding enterprise and skill in piloting aircraft during hazardous aircraft trials".

Brown is credited with at least two important firsts in carrier aviation, both in 1945. In April he conducted the first aircraft carrier landing in an aircraft with a tricycle undercarriage, and in December 1945, Brown became the first pilot to land on and take-off from a carrier in a jet aircraft (almost all aircraft at the time were propeller-driven). The aircraft he flew for this second feat is now on display at the Fleet Air Arm Museum in Yeovilton, Somerset.

As the Second World War drew to a close, Brown was tasked with acquiring and assessing German aviation technology, before it could be destroyed. He was an ideal choice for the job, due to the combination of his unparalleled flight experience and his fluency in German.

By the end of the war, German aircraft technology had become the best in the world – their jet- and rocket-powered aircraft had no direct match in the Allied arsenal. Brown was shocked at how advanced the German technology had become, and was given opportunities to test fly these creations. This included the new, rocket-propelled Messerschmitt Me 163 Komet – a lethal prototype and vision of the future of high-powered flight.

On one such mission, Brown headed for a Luftwaffe airbase in Denmark. German forces were in retreat from Denmark at the time but, unbeknown to Brown, the Allied troops had not yet reached the airbase. Fortunately, the German commanding officer surrendered the base and its 2,000 men to Brown, and the Allied forces arrived the next day.

Due to his fluency in German, Brown was also tasked with interviewing Nazis. He was present at the liberation of Bergen-Belsen concentration camp, where he was asked to interrogate the head guards. This included camp Commandant Josef Kramer and 22-year-old female commander Irma Grese, nicknamed the 'beautiful beast of Belsen'.

Speaking to the BBC in 2013, Brown described her as "the worst human being I have ever met". "Her cruelty in Auschwitz was unbelievable," he said. "She was the one who made lampshades from the skins of prisoners and that sort of thing... We never got anything out of her at all. She didn't seem to have any feeling at all about human beings."

Both Kramer and Grese were later tried and hanged for war crimes.

Brown also interrogated top-ranking Nazis Hermann Göring and Heinrich Himmler, both of whom had been responsible for managing the Nazi concentration camps. Brown said that after their interview, Göring offered his hand to Brown. "I couldn't under any circumstances shake it. I thought, 'what the hell do I do now?'" Rather than shaking hands, and aware that Göring had a respect for pilots, Brown responded "Hals- und Beinbruch" – the same German fighter pilot greeting that WWI fighter ace Udet had given Brown in 1936.

Brown described Himmler as a "snivelling coward". "He was so frightened of what would happen to him. It was all aimed at saving his own skin," he said.

After WWII, Brown was put in charge of the Enemy Aircraft Flight, an elite group of pilots who test-flew captured German aircraft. Through this and other experiences he is said to have flown almost every type of plane that was involved in the Second World War, and therefore one of the few people qualified to compare Allied and Axis aeroplanes.

In 1946 jet aircraft were evolving rapidly. The race was on to master jet-powered flight, and to break the sound barrier. Brown flew the prototype de Havilland DH.108 jet aircraft – both his predecessor and his successor were killed in accidents while flying variants of this plane. Brown narrowly escaped a similar fate, escaping from a Mach 0.88 dive which went badly wrong. "The ride was smooth, then suddenly it all went to pieces... as the plane porpoised wildly my chin hit my chest, jerked hard back, slammed forward again, repeated it over and over, flogged by the awful whipping of the plane..." Brown managed to pull back gently on both stick and throttle and regain control of the aircraft. Only three DH.108 aircraft were made, and all were lost in fatal accidents.

During the Korean War in the '50s, Brown worked as a trainer with the United States Naval Test Pilot School. By 1960 Brown had been promoted to Captain, and in 1970 he retired and was appointed Commander of the Order of the British Empire (CBE). He finally stopped flying aged 70.

Captain Brown's career saw him become one of Britain's most highly regarded pilots. He began his flying career in a biplane, and ended up flying supersonic jet Typhoons in the 1960s. It's estimated that Brown escaped a total of 15 near-fatal air incidents during his career. He put his survival down, in part, to his short stature.

His world record for flying the greatest number of different aircraft still stands (487, not including the many variants of models that he flew as part of his test role). He also holds the record for the most carrier landings (2,407). He met Winston Churchill and King George VI several times, even once crashing in front of Churchill. He also became good friends with Neil Armstrong, the first person to walk on the moon (as well as being an astronaut, Armstrong had also been a test pilot and it was he that approached Brown, aware of his reputation and feats).

There are many fascinating details to Captain Eric Brown's story, too many to include here. So, to any readers who wish to learn more, we urge you to read Brown's autobiography, 'Wings on My Sleeve' (the updated version from 2007), which gives detailed insights into his remarkable and unique life.

reddit referrer: AlDente

Hessy Taft

Nazi propaganda's 'perfect Aryan' poster child was actually Jewish

When Hessy Taft's parents, Jacob and Pauline Levinsons, moved to Berlin in 1928 as a newly wedded Jewish couple hoping to pursue singing careers, anti-Semitism was already on the rise. By the time Taft's mother gave birth to a beautiful daughter in 1934, the city had already fallen dangerously under Nazi influence.

Six months later, in 1935, Taft's mother took her wide-eyed baby to a renowned photographer to have a portrait made. Thinking the portrait to be a private family photograph, Taft's parents framed the picture and displayed it on their piano. But not long after, a housekeeper exclaimed at the sight of the portrait and rushed from their house, returning with a copy of the Nazi family magazine, 'Sonne ins Hause'. The front cover image was the portrait of little Hessy.

Her mother went straight to the photographer and demanded to know how a picture of her Jewish daughter had ended up on the front page of a Nazi magazine. The photographer explained that he had entered the photograph into a Nazi contest that was looking for the perfect Aryan child to be the poster child for their propaganda regime. He said that he had known

Hessy was Jewish and had "wanted to make the Nazis ridiculous". Evidently his trick had worked. Apparently Joseph Goebbels himself, the Nazi propaganda minister, had personally chosen Hessy's portrait from a great number of submissions.

Taft's portrait was printed all over Nazi postcards and posters, advertising the 'perfect Aryan child' but although the photographer was enjoying his joke, Taft's mother was too afraid that her Jewish daughter would be recognised to take her out of the house. Eventually the Levinsons family was forced to flee Nazi Germany, settling first in Latvia, then Paris, and finally escaping to Cuba with the help of the French Resistance.

Now in her eighties, Hessy Taft is a professor of chemistry in New York. In an interview with the German newspaper *Bild*, she said, "I can laugh about it now, but if the Nazis had known who I really was, I wouldn't be alive."

reddit referrer: Battle4Seattle

Hubert Rochereau

French WWI soldier whose room remains unchanged since 1918

Hubert Rochereau was one of millions who fought and lost their lives in the Great War. A French second lieutenant with the 15th Dragoons Regiment based in Libourne, his death came on 26 April 1918 due to injuries he sustained fighting in the village of Loker, Belgium.

Rochereau posthumously received military decorations – the *Croix de Guerre*, and the Legion of Honour for his extreme bravery on the battlefield.

Memorials exist all across Europe to the Great War's many casualties; however, Rochereau's memorial is a bit different.

Rochereau's parents decided to keep their son's room unchanged from the day he left their house for the final time.

When they finally decide to move house in 1935, a condition of the sale was that the room remained 'as is' for 500 years.

The room is essentially 'frozen in time' – a snapshot of a bygone era, now beyond living memory. Rochereau's bed, decorations, clothes, furniture and military memorabilia – even his pipe and tobacco – are all preserved.

On the desk is a vial, its label reads: "the soil of Flanders on which our dear child fell and which has kept his remains for four years".

The current owner of the house, Daniel Fabre, told the Nouvelle République newspaper that the 500-year clause "had no legal basis". However, he and his wife continue to honour the wishes set down by Hubert Rochereau's parents.

reddit referrer: mosestrod

Irena Sendler

Saviour of over 2,500 children

Oskar Schindler is rightly praised for saving 1,200
Jewish lives during the Holocaust, and the Steven
Spielberg movie made him a globally recognised hero.
Far fewer people, however, have ever heard of Irena
Sendler. She smuggled 2,500 Jewish children from the
Warsaw Ghetto, by whatever means possible, and –
again like Schindler – risked her own life in the process.

As a Roman Catholic Social Worker, Sendler was put
in charge of the children's department of Zegota, the
Council for Aid to Jews. As part of her work, she had a
permit allowing her to enter the Warsaw Ghetto to check
for any signs of typhoid, as the Nazis were worried this
would spread across the city and beyond. She was also
allowed to administer vaccinations against typhoid,
and give other medication. However, during these visits,
Sendler would wear a Star of David so as not to draw
attention to herself, and in order to gain trust from the
Jewish population.

Realising the severity of the situation, Irena made
the decision to do all she could to save as many children
as possible. Small children and babies were smuggled
out in a variety of ways, ranging from being hidden in
ambulances or suitcases to being disguised as packages,

or being led to safety through the underground sewer systems.

The children were placed in orphanages or convents, or occasionally with families who were sympathetic, with the help of around 300 volunteers aiding safe arrival and placements. In order for the children to not be suspected of being Jewish, they were taught Christian prayers. Sendler kept a record of the name of every child who was safely rescued, with the intention that they would be reunited with their families after the war.

In October 1943, the Gestapo raided Irena's house. Her immediate concern was to remove the list with details of the children, so she threw it out of the window to a colleague, who hid it in her underwear. Irena was then taken to Pawaik Prison, where her legs and feet were broken, and her body severely scarred. Despite this, she did not release any details about the children saved. She was sentenced to death by firing squad, but evaded execution when another member of Zegota bribed one of the guards to release her.

Sendler then buried the list of names in a jar underneath an apple tree in a friend's garden, and continued her work. For the rest of the war, she lived in hiding, under a different identity.

Sadly, after the war her attempts to reunite children with their families were largely unsuccessful, as she discovered that most of the families had been sent to the gas chambers at Treblinka concentration camp.

Although not a household name outside Poland or Israel, Sendler's achievements did not go unnoticed. In 1965 Sendler was recognized by Israel's official memorial to the victims of the Holocaust, Yad Vashem, as one of the 'Righteous among the Nations'. In 2003 she received the Order of the White Eagle, Poland's highest civilian decoration, and in 2007 Polish President Lech Kaczynski said she could "justly be nominated for the Nobel Peace Prize".

Despite Sendler's remarkable success in saving so many lives, she was haunted by the memories of those she couldn't save. "We who were rescuing children are not some kind of heroes... I could have done more. This regret will follow me to my death."

Irena Sendler died in May 2008, aged 98.

Also see *Chiune Sugihara.*

reddit referrer: megster53

Joseph Beyrle

The only American soldier to have served with both the
United States Army and the Soviet Army in World War II

A US Army enlistee during World War II, Michigan-
born Joseph Beyrle became a paratrooper with the 101st
Airborne's Screaming Eagles.

His first two missions involved parachuting into
France to deliver gold to the French resistance.

On the night before D-Day, Beyrle parachuted into
Normandy, France; his mission to blow up two bridges.
Three days later he was captured by the Germans, and
on the way to a prison camp his dog tags were taken,
and placed on another man's corpse. When the body was
found, Beyrle's mother was notified prematurely of her
son's death.

Beyrle was taken to a number of German prison
camps, beaten and starved. Though he managed to
escape twice, he was caught both times. After the second
escape he was handed over to the Gestapo, who planned
to shoot him as they believed he was a spy.

Taken to the Stalag III prisoner of war camp he
learned that the Soviet Red Army were only a few miles
away. His next escape was successful, and he managed
to reach Soviet troops, fighting alongside them for over
a month, as a gunner on a Sherman tank. Coincidentally,

the battalion's commander was the legendary Alexandra Samusenko, thought to be the only female tank officer of that rank in WWII.

The Soviets managed to make use of Beyrle's demolition skills, and he even took part in the freeing of his old POW camp. A couple of weeks later, an attack by German Stuka dive bombers left him seriously wounded, and he was taken to a field hospital. Whilst there he was visited by Soviet Marshal Georgy Zhukov, who provided him with official papers in order to rejoin the American forces.

Joining a Soviet military convoy, Beyrle arrived at the US embassy in Moscow in February 1945, where he discovered that he had been reported as killed in action in 1944. A funeral mass had been held for him in his home town of Muskegon, and his obituary was published in the local newspaper. Officers in Moscow placed him under guard in the Metropol Hotel until his identity was established with his fingerprints.

After the war, Beyrle returned to Muskegon, where he worked as a supervisor for the Brunswick Corp, maker of bowling balls and pool tables. He retired in 1981.

In a 1994 ceremony at the White House, marking the 50th anniversary of D-Day, Beyrle received medals from both US President Bill Clinton and the Russian President Boris Yeltsin. His son John Beyrle remarked that "It was the proudest moment of his life".

Beyrle died in his sleep in December 2004 during a visit to Toccoa, Georgia, the same town where he had trained with the paratroopers in 1942.

reddit referrer: SamadhiBlue

Nancy Wake

The Gestapo's most wanted, for evading capture so many times

Nancy Wake was a British Agent in WWII, where she evaded capture so many times that she was known as the 'White Mouse', and by 1943 had become the Gestapo's most wanted, with a price of 5 million francs on her head.

Living in France when it fell in 1940, Nancy subsequently became a part of the French Resistance. Her initial duties involved organising supplies of ammunition and arms, and being in control of finances. She was also given the responsibility of helping allied soldiers escape from German-occupied France.

After this, Nancy was head of a troop of resistance fighters who were to destroy bridges and railways in an effort to make communication and transport more difficult for the Germans. This led to running frequent attacks on Gestapo Headquarters, including with a troop of 7,000 resistance fighters against 22,000 Gestapo, with the Gestapo suffering more injuries than her troops.

On another occasion, she had destroyed the codes in her wireless operator due to a Gestapo raid, and in order to replace them, cycled through many German checkpoints in a 500km journey which took her over

71 hours to complete. By this time, there was a 5 million francs price on her head and the Gestapo were attempting to find her, meaning it was even more of an achievement to survive this journey.

Nancy was arrested once, due to being one of a group suspected over a bomb, but she was rescued by another member of the resistance, who pretended her lack of alibi was because she was his mistress, and so the police let her go. Whilst she had not been involved in this case, she did commit many murders, including killing an SS member with her bare hands. As Nancy herself said, "In my opinion, the only good German was a dead German, and the deader, the better. I killed a lot of Germans, and I am only sorry I didn't kill more." When asking whether she was ever afraid in these situations, Nancy replied, "Hah! I've never been afraid in my life."

reddit referrer: godsenfrik

Peggy Harris

Widow found her husband was being commemorated 60 years after his death

Woman who searched for her husband, a pilot reported missing in WWII, for over 60 years and finally found that he was being commemorated every year by the residents of a small Normandy town.

Billie Harris and his wife Peggy Harris had only been married for six weeks when Billie was called away to fly in France in WWII. In his final letter to his newly wedded wife, he said he would be home as soon as space became available on a ship. While flying over Normandy on 17th July 1944 though, Billie's plane was shot down and he never caught a ship home. Information regarding his death and burial was delivered to Peggy in confused and often conflicting accounts. But for more than 60 years, Peggy never gave up trying to find out where her husband had fallen and been buried.

Finally, Billie's cousin Alton requested Billie's military records and was told that a woman in France had also asked for them and had received copies. Peggy and Alton contacted the woman, who they found to be living in a small town in Normandy called Les Ventes, and flew out to see her. There they were shocked to discover that the town's main road had been named after Billie and that he had been honoured every year for 60 years by a march through the town.

Peggy was told that during his fatal fall from the skies, Billie had deliberately steered his plane into a forest to avoid crashing into the town.

Peggy now sends flowers to his gravestone ten times a year to celebrate various anniversaries.

reddit referrer: Allformygain

Simo Häyhä

'White Death', the greatest sniper ever?

WWII Finnish soldier Simo Häyhä holds the macabre, yet nonetheless incredible, record for the highest number of confirmed kills by any sniper in any war.

With a natural talent for sharp-shooting, as a youth Häyhä accrued numerous marksmanship trophies. In the mid 1920s he served a 15 month stint in the Finnish army, before going back to his regular life of farming and hunting.

Then came the Second World War. In what became known as the 'Winter War', the Soviets invaded Finland in 1939. The Finns were hugely outnumbered and outgunned. Like many other Finns keen to protect their homeland, Häyhä reported for duty.

Dressed head-to-toe in white camouflage, and operating in temperatures between -40 C and -20°C, Häyhä and his fellow Finns used guerrilla tactics to fight the Soviets. Small teams would travel cross country on skis, often at night and in silence, isolating and ambushing pockets of Soviet soldiers who were often confined to travel by road due to their tanks and heavy equipment. The Battle of Kolloa was the site of much of the most intense fighting, with the battle lasting until the end of the war. It was here that Häyhä made his mark as a sniper.

Häyhä favoured a bolt action rifle with iron sights, rather than the usual telescopic sights on most sniper rifles. This meant he had a lower profile than other snipers as his head didn't need to be raised quite so high. A lack of telescopic sight scope also meant there were no reflections that could reveal his location to enemy snipers (a technique he used to great effect to locate Soviet snipers). To further conceal his position, he often ate snow in an effort to prevent the moisture in his warm breath.

By the end of the war, Häyhä was credited with 505 confirmed kills, although some sources claim the actual total was 542. Even more remarkable is that he achieved all this in under 100 days, averaging just over five kills per day – at a time of year with very few daylight hours. His 'personal best' was 25 Soviet soldiers in a single day. "I just shot every time I saw an enemy. I didn't care if he was a commander or not," Häyhä remarked.

In addition to his sniper kills, Häyhä also killed another couple of hundred with a Suomi 9mm machine gun bringing his total for the 'Winter War' to almost 800 kills. Häyhä became a wartime celebrity with newspapers celebrating his high kill count.

So feared was he that the Soviets referred to him as the 'Belaya Smert' ('White Death'). They tried repeatedly to kill him, using methods such as counter-snipers and artillery strikes. Finally, on 6 March 1940, a Russian soldier shot Häyhä with an exploding bullet, in the lower left jaw. These bullets, nicknamed 'dumdums', had been banned in the St Petersburg Declaration of 1868.

Fellow soldiers who found him said "half his cheek was missing". Although seriously wounded and left in a coma, Häyhä survived. He regained consciousness several days later – incidentally on the day peace was declared. A new jaw was crafted for Häyhä from a piece of his hip bone. His rifle was left at the battlefield and never seen again.

When the war ended, Häyhä was promoted from Corporal to Second Lieutenant. In 1961 the Finnish government gave him his own farm and between 1962 and 1966 he won the Ruokolahti Hunting Society's Game Cup five times in a row.

Simo Häyhä died in 2002, aged 96. His remarkable record has never been surpassed, and in many ways that's no bad thing.

Häyhä's self-declared secret to his extraordinary marksmanship? "Practice."

reddit referrer: Kamon2011

Stanislaw Jerzy Lec

Survived a German concentration camp by killing guard with the shovel he was supposed to dig his own grave with

The Polish poet and aphorist immortalised his stunning escape from a German camp in the Second World War in one of his most famous poems, *He who had dug his own grave*.

Lec was under a death sentence for trying to escape previously from the camp at Ternopol, and was given a shovel to dig his own grave. Instead, he killed the guard with it and used the guard's uniform to disguise himself for his escape.

His successful attempt to escape the camp in 1943 was actually his third attempt.

Born the son of a baron in 1909 in Lemberg, then part of the Austro-Hungarian Empire, Lec moved with his family to Vienna when the Great War broke out in 1914, but returned to the town of his birth (now renamed Lwow in the Second Polish Republic) after the war.

Lec made his literary debut in 1929, with much of his work appearing in left-wing and communist magazines, and he co-founded a satirical magazine in 1935. His work has been translated into several languages, including English, German and Italian.

He was given a state funeral in Warsaw when he died in May 1966.

reddit referrer: Ska-doosh

Vasili Arkhipov

Saving the world from World War Three

Vasili Arkhipov stopped the launch of a nuclear torpedo in the Cuban Missile Crisis, which would, very likely, have led to a nuclear war.

A Soviet Navy officer at the time, Vasili was on the Soviet submarine B-59 on 27th October 1962, when it was shot at by US surface ships. The B-59 submarine was hiding from the US ships which were pursuing it, so had not been in contact with Moscow for a number of days, and had also not been able to pick up radio signals because of the depth it was at. Due to this, the Captain, Valentin Grigorievitch Savitsky, believed that the shots fired nearby were a sign that a war had begun, which they did not know about because their location prevented them receiving any information. There was a nuclear missile on board the B-59, and Captain Savitsky ordered it to be launched in retaliation to the previous shots, which he had falsely assumed were proof that war had begun.

However, in order for any nuclear weapon to be launched, the most important three Soviets on the submarine needed to have a unanimous vote. Political Officer Ivan Semonovich Maslennikov agreed with Captain Savitsky, and was in favour of the missile being launched. Vasili was the third member whose opinion had to be taken into consideration, and he did not want the missile to be launched. After intense debate, Vasili persuaded Ivan that launching the missile would not be beneficial. Captain Savitsky was unimpressed with this decision, but could not act without the support of the other two, and the submarine resurfaced. If the missile had been launched, the US would almost certainly have retaliated, and it is highly probable that nuclear war would have resulted. Robert McNamara, the US Secretary of Defense during the Cuban Missile Crisis, said that this event bought the countries "closer than we knew at the time" to nuclear war. Vasili's decision to not launch the weapon potentially prevented the beginning of World War Three.

reddit referrer: interpellation

William Patrick Hitler

Adolf Hitler's nephew begged President Roosevelt to allow him to join the Allied forces

In 1942, Adolf Hitler's nephew, William Patrick Hitler, wrote a letter to the president of the United States, Franklin D Roosevelt. In this letter he asked to be allowed to fight with the Allied forces against his "ill-famed" uncle whose regime he described as "devilish and pagan".

William Hitler escaped Nazi Germany in 1939 and fled to Britain where he made his first pleas to be permitted to fight with the British forces. He was turned down for reasons he later described to Roosevelt in his letter as because the British people, "while they are kind and courteous...could not in the long run feel overly cordial or sympathetic towards an individual bearing the name I do". He also described how the English legal system would not allow him to change his name without great expense, which he was unable to afford.

In 1940, soon after Adolf Hitler invaded France and the first doomed trains returned empty from Auschwitz concentration camp, William Hitler moved across the Atlantic to New York City to try and persuade the US forces to accept him among their ranks and to express his desire "to see active combat as soon as possible and thereby be accepted by [his] friends and comrades as one of them in this great struggle for liberty".

In his letter, he outlines the ways in which he had already rebelled against his uncle, saying, "As a fugitive from the Gestapo, I warned France through the press that Hitler would invade her that year. The people of England I warned by the same means that the so-called 'solution' of Munich was a myth that would bring terrible consequences." He recalls his frustration at his Cassandrian task but stresses that he continued "to do those things which as a Christian [he] knew to be right".

Roosevelt was so persuaded by William Hitler's words that he passed his letter on to FBI director J Edgar Hoover who accepted him into the Allied forces. For three years William Hitler fought against his uncle, by whom he was referred to as "my loathsome nephew", until he was discharged due to injury. He returned to the United States where he changed his name to William Stuart-Houston, married and had four children. He lived there until his death in 1987.

reddit referer: LegendaryBlue

Yang Kyoungjong

World War II soldier who was forced to fight for the Japanese, the Soviets and the Germans

When American paratroopers landed in Normandy in June 1944 after D-Day, they thought they had captured a Japanese soldier wearing a German uniform. It turned out the soldier was Korean, and his involvement in the war was probably unique.

Korean Yang Kyoungjong was forcibly conscripted at the age of 18 by the Japanese in 1938. At the time, Korea was ruled by Japan and Kyoungjong was taken to fight the Soviet Red Army. During the Battles of Khalkhin Gol in 1939, he was captured by the Soviet Red Army camp.

The Soviets were low on manpower due to their heavy fighting with Nazi Germany, so in 1942 Kyoungjong was again forcibly conscripted – this time for the Soviets – along with thousands of other prisoners.

In 1943, he was captured by German soldiers in Ukraine, and was then forced into fighting for Germany. Kyoungjong was sent to Occupied France to serve in the 'Eastern Battalion' with other Soviet prisoners of war. After the D-Day landings in Normandy by the Allied forces in June 1944, Kyoungjong was captured one final time – by paratroopers of the United States Army.

He was sent to a prison camp in Britain, followed

by a camp in the United States. After the end of the war, Kyoungjong settled in Illinois where he lived until his death in 1992.

See also: Joseph Beyrle

reddit referrer: lappy482

SCIENCE

"Should we force science down the throats of those that have no taste for it? Is it our duty to drag them kicking and screaming into the twenty-first century? I am afraid that it is."

– George Porter

Clyde Tombaugh

Discoverer of Pluto – his ashes are on their way to the planet

The man who discovered Pluto in 1930 is set to make his mark posthumously as his ashes are on their way to the outermost planet in the solar system.

The New Horizons spacecraft is set to reach Pluto in July 2015, having blasted off from Cape Canaveral on a nine-year journey covering three billion miles.

Clyde Tombaugh, the only American to discover a planet in the solar system, died in 1997. At the time scientists were trying to secure funds for a first space mission to Pluto. They argued that the mission needed to be undertaken before the planet moved away from its favourable position, further away from the sun, and its surface became more frozen. The planet has a long orbit of 248 years.

The plan is for New Horizons to get within 10,000km of Pluto's surface, and 27,000km from its large moon Charon, and make use of its three cameras (for visible light, infrared and ultraviolet images) and three spectrometers for images and analysis. The mission will continue past Pluto, into the Kuiper Belt, a large region of icy planetoids.

The nuclear-powered spacecraft set off from Florida

in January 2006 and just over a year later passed Jupiter, using the planet's gravity to speed up the craft's journey using a slingshot effect. It traversed the orbit of Neptune in August 2014, the last major crossing before Pluto.

New Horizons is on the fastest trip ever to the outer solar system. It reached the Earth's moon's orbit in just nine hours. Weighing half a ton with its full load of fuel, and measuring about eight feet wide, the probe is now well on its way to its historic encounter with Tombaugh's Pluto. A radio signal, moving at the speed of light, will take about four hours to reach Earth from Pluto; the world awaits.

reddit referrer: seven7hwave

Dr Norman Borlaug

**Plant scientist credited with saving over
a billion people during his lifetime**

Norman Borlaug started his incredible career at the
University of Minnesota where he received a BSc in
Biology in 1937, and a PhD in Plant Pathology and
Genetics in 1942. On receipt of his PhD, Dr Borlaug
spent time in Mexico studying crop growth and
development and was shocked at the conditions he
discovered there. He wrote to his wife, "These places
I've seen have clubbed my mind — they are so poor and
depressing. I don't know what we can do to help these
people, but we've got to do something."

Borlaug had set his heart on helping the poor to
feed themselves and, along with his team, he spent a
great deal of time toiling to improve crop resistance to
disease and to increase yield. When he had developed a
grain that he believed to be better suited to the Mexican
climate, Borlaug began to introduce the newly developed
grain to Mexican agriculture and, by 1963, Mexico had
become a net exporter of wheat. Borlaug extended his
efforts to other countries for whom famine was a very
real threat and between 1965 and 1970 wheat yield in
Pakistan and India had doubled, banishing the imminent
threat of hunger in a way no one had dreamed was

possible. Mexico and India's self-sufficiency is accredited to Borlaug's determined work.

In 1970, as Borlaug toiled under the hot Mexican sun in his on-going determination to develop more sustainable and higher-yielding crops for poor nations, his wife sought him out to tell him the news that he had been awarded the Nobel Peace Prize, to which he replied, "Someone's pulling your leg." But he was wrong. The Nobel Prize committee said on his achievement: "More than any other single person of this age, he has helped provide bread for a hungry world. We have made this choice in the hope that providing bread will also give the world peace."

For his tireless efforts, Borlaug was also awarded the Presidential Medal of Freedom, the Congressional Gold Medal and the Padma Vibhushan, India's second highest civilian honour. He has been dubbed 'The father of the Green Revolution', 'Agriculture's greatest spokesperson' and 'The man who saved a billion lives'. It is believed that, on average, his breakthroughs saved 10.5 million people a year during his lifetime.

Dr Borlaug died in 2009, aged 95, but he will always be remembered as a man who spent his whole life striving to help those less fortunate than himself.

reddit referrer: timopod5

Elizabeth Holmes

Invented a method to run 200 tests on a drop of blood

In 2003, aged just 19, Stanford student Elizabeth Holmes made a courageous move. Approaching her Stanford professor, she suggested that they start a company together.

Holmes wasn't a typical student. As a teenager she had learned Mandarin in her own time, and by college age she was filing her own patents. Her college professor recognised a unique talent so, after some negotiation, Holmes finally managed to convince him that leaving college and setting up a new company was a good idea.

Speaking to Fortune in 2014, Holmes' former professor explained his thinking when he was convinced about her abilities: "When I finally connected with what Elizabeth fundamentally is," he said, "I realised that I could have just as well have been looking into the eyes of a Steve Jobs or Bill Gates."

Holmes dropped out of Stanford and, using her college money, founded her own company, 'Theranos', of which she is CEO (the company name is an amalgamation of 'therapy' and 'diagnosis').

Then began Holmes' research and development for a completely new method for blood testing. Ten years, 500 employees and $400 million in investment later,

Theranos launched its new, rapid diagnosis, blood testing technique.

With only a few drops of blood, more than 200 tests can be carried out. Even a single drop of 50 microlitres can be used to conduct in excess of 70 tests. Equivalent conventional tests require hundreds of times more blood. Using the new technique, results are usually available within a few hours.

Perhaps the most significant benefit of Theranos' new technique is its relatively low cost – sometimes just ten percent that of traditional techniques. The effect could be dramatic, saving billions of dollars in the US alone, and offering the potential of more accessible, cheaper blood testing globally. In 2014 Theranos began rolling out their testing centres in the US, with plans to expand into Europe and beyond.

reddit referrer: aeo1003

Henrietta Lacks

The first immortal human?

Henrietta Lacks died in 1951. However, she is possibly the closest any has come to achieving immortality.

Doctors removed some of Henrietta Lacks' cells before her death, and they have been used in a multiplicity of countries.

Henrietta was an uneducated black woman, who died of cervical cancer. However, before her death, doctors removed some of her cells, which have been used in many countries ever since. Whilst being treated for her tumour, two samples of her cervix were removed without her permission. These were taken by Dr George Otto Gey, who proceeded to culture them, and create the immortal HeLa cell line. Due to the durability of Henrietta's cells, they have become the most commonly used human cell line in biomedicine, proving important for research and treatment. They are also the first cells to be successfully cloned, and more than 74,000 studies have been based on results found from them.

Henrietta's descendants had no idea that her cells were being used for this purpose until 1973, when they were contacted asking for blood samples to be used in experiments in conjuncture with the HeLa cell line. It was not until recently that this caused problems, however, when the genome sequence of Henrietta's cells was publicly produced, meaning it could be seen by anyone. The Lacks family had not been informed of this decision, and their permission had not been asked. Their concern was to do with privacy, as they did not know what information about their grandmother was being published, and also how information from the genetic sequence could show things about the rest of the family. The National Institute of Health reached an agreement with the Lacks family, which does not give them any financial benefit, but does allow them control over what research HeLa genes are used in, and who is able to see the results. The case of 'immortal' Henrietta Lacks shows the ethical dilemmas which often need to be taken into consideration in medical research.

reddit referrer: linkittogether

Henrietta Leavitt

Unsung hero of astronomy

The early twentieth century was a fast-moving time
for astronomy. Breakthroughs and discoveries were
expanding human understanding of the universe, and
astronomers were benefiting from the development
of ever-more-powerful telescopes. However a key
problem was how to measure the distance of a star, from
Earth. Without the ability to measure basic distances,
understanding of the universe was severely limited.

Enter Henrietta Leavitt, a lesser-known contributor
to this period of growth in scientific understanding.

A graduate of Radcliffe College, Leavitt worked at
Harvard Observatory from 1895, employed in its great
project: determining the brightness of stars. Initially
tasked with counting stars on photographic plates,
Leavitt was evidently highly intelligent and was later
promoted to head of the photographic stellar photometry
department. She was tasked with making best use of the
new photographic techniques which were revolutionising
astronomy.

It had been known for centuries that the apparent
brightness of an object decreases as the square of its
distance – known as the 'inverse square law of light
brightness'. 'Intrinsic brightness' is how bright it actually

is, and 'apparent brightness' how bright it appears to an observer. If you know both the apparent and intrinsic brightness of a star, you can calculate how far from Earth it is.

Leavitt focused on variable stars – stars whose apparent brightness fluctuates – called Cepheids. She showed that some of the Cepheids showed a pattern – the brighter ones appeared to have longer pulsation periods and the relationship was quite close and predictable. Put simply, the Cepheids' pulses are related to their average intrinsic brightness.

This discovery – the period-luminosity relation – was critical as it allowed the intrinsic brightness of the star to be calculated. By comparing a Cepheid's apparent brightness with its intrinsic brightness, astronomers were able to determine the star's distance, using the inverse square law of light brightness.

Leavitt's discovery enabled astronomers to use the Cepheids as 'yardsticks' to measure distances from Earth to other stars and galaxies. For instance, Edwin Hubble used this method to prove that spiral nebulae are in fact distant galaxies.

Throughout her career, Leavitt discovered more than 2,400 variable stars, about half of the known total at the time. Her achievements are made even more remarkable by the fact that Leavitt was deaf following an illness shortly after graduation.

Due to the prejudices of the early twentieth century, Leavitt was not able to pursue her own study areas, and was obliged to research whatever the head of the observatory assigned. Leavitt's talents were never fully realised, but a colleague described her as "possessing the best mind at the Observatory".

In the 1990s, the Hubble Space Telescope was used to refine measurements of extragalactic distances. To do so they pointed it at the Cepheids.

reddit referrer: costheta

Jamie Edwards

The world's youngest amateur nuclear scientist

Lots of teenagers have hobbies. For some, football holds the key; for others, electric guitar, or perhaps games consoles. Yet for a 13 year-old school student, nuclear physics was the only way to go.

The world's youngest *'amateur nuclear physicist'* and newest *'fusioneer'*, Jamie Edwards from Preston in England was first inspired to dabble in nuclear physics after reading the exploits of another young scientist, Tyler Wilson, who, at the age of 14, created his first fusion reactor in his garden garage.

Fusion, Jamie reminds us, is the complex process of 'smashing together' a number of atoms of a smaller nuclear number into a single atom of a larger nuclear number, using a fusion reactor. This whole process is performed within a vacuum, using strong magnetic fields to heat the charged particles, giving them enough energy to properly 'fuse'. The process is most famously seen in our own Sun. As Jamie playfully notes, fusion is really just the art of making "a star in a jar".

Suitably inspired, Jamie approached his classmates and teacher with the idea of undertaking his own fusion project at school – the attempt to fuse Hydrogen atoms to create Helium. After repeated assurance to his

243

headmaster that the experiment would not blow up the building, and to his great delight, Jamie was given the go ahead.

With a little start up money from his school (given, quite possibly, with a small measure of trepidation) as well as generous donations from an interested public, and help from the professional *R&B Switchgear Group*, Jamie allowed excited onlookers to join him on his online blog, as he documented the highs and lows of creating a fusion reactor. The internet sympathised as a damaged cooling fan slowed down the project and delayed attempted fusion, held its breath as the machine was tested, and celebrated as Hydrogen atoms were successfully fused, cheering with Jamie as he plainly noted: "Yesterday I successfully achieved fusion at 11.30 am."

As a promising potential solution to the energy problems the world currently faces, any advancement in fusion research is a truly exciting development. Though the field remains largely locked in the theoretical, it is the next generation of scientists, exemplified by Jamie, who likely hold the key. For now, at least, the world's youngest nuclear physicist has opened the door for budding scientists to follow in his footsteps; the *R&B Switchgear Group* having been inspired to create a £10,000 budget in the name of young scientists, trying

their hand at changing history. The fund is aptly named –
The Star in a Jar Fund.

reddit referrer: SweatyBaws

Lene Hau

Faster than light, master of light

Danish scientist Lene Hau can travel faster than light. That sentence may sound like hyperbole, but it's true. Hau achieved this incredible feat, not with a spaceship or new propulsion technology, but by slowing the speed that light travels.

The 'speed of light' – 186,282 miles per second – is actually light's maximum speed, and it only holds true in a vacuum. When light travels through any substance, its speed is slowed. For example, in water, light travels at 'only' 140,000 miles per second.

Hau is a professor of physics at Harvard. In 1999, she and her colleagues slowed light to an incredible 38 miles an hour. This was achieved by passing a laser beam of light through a Bose-Einstein condensate – a tiny 0.1mm cloud of atoms. The cloud was suspended magnetically in a vacuum chamber which had been cooled to within a billionth of a degree of absolute zero – the coldest place in the universe.

"It's nifty to look into the chamber and see a clump of ultracold atoms floating there," Hau says. "In this odd state, light takes on a more human dimension; you can almost touch it."

Hau then took this a step further by not just slowing

light but fully stopping it, and then – amazingly – restarting it.

"Two years ago we slowed it down to 38 miles an hour; now we've been able to park it then bring it back up to full speed," Hau told the Harvard University Gazette in 2001.

As if that weren't enough, things then got head-scratchingly weird in 2006. This time Hau stopped light, transferred it into matter, moved it, then converted it back to light.

To do this the Bose-Einstein condensate was converted into a hologram, a sort of matter version of the pulse. Then Hau and her team transferred that matter waveform into an entirely different Bose-Einstein condensate nearby — which, a fraction of a second later, emitted the original light pulse. The results were published in *Nature*.

Of its potential, Hau said: "While the matter is travelling between the two Bose–Einstein condensates, we can trap it, potentially for minutes, and reshape it – change it – in whatever way we want. This novel form of quantum control could also have applications in the developing fields of quantum information processing and quantum cryptography."

Although not a household name, Hau has won numerous awards for her work, including the George

Ledlie Prize, and 'World Dane 2010'.

Harvard's Provost Steven Hyman prasied Hau: "Her work is path-breaking. Her research blurs the boundaries between basic and applied science, draws on the talent and people of two Schools and several departments, and provides a literally glowing example of how taking daring intellectual risks leads to profound rewards."

reddit referrer: Tamnegripe

Mary Anning

Contribution to science recognised a century and a half after her death

A fossil collector and palaeontologist who lived in the first half of the nineteenth century, Mary Anning's contribution to scientific thinking about prehistoric life on Earth was significant yet never fully recognised during her life. Indeed she was so shunned by the scientific community, she said "the world has used me so unkindly".

Mary's mistake in life, apart from being poor, was to be born a woman, and therefore ineligible to join the Geographical Society of London (which didn't admit women until 1904) and generally not receiving official recognition for any of her scientific discoveries. Despite this, she sold her fossils worldwide and was consulted on issues of anatomy, including corresponding with geologist Charles Lyell, a close friend of Charles Darwin.

Mary made many important fossil findings along the Jurassic coast in Dorset, England, including the first ichthyosaur skeleton to be identified and other important fish fossils.

Posthumously she finally achieved recognition of her significant contribution when Charles Dickens wrote about her in 1865, and in 2010 she was named in the

Royal Society's list of the ten most influential women in the history of science. She also lives on in the well-known tongue-twister: 'she sells seashells by the seashore'.

reddit user: user's account no longer active

Index

INDEX

INDEX

INDEX

INDEX

INDEX

INDEX